FIRE
AND RAIN

FIRE
AND RAIN
THE WILD-HEARTED
FAITH OF ELIJAH

RAY PRITCHARD

Nashville, Tennessee

ISBN: 978-0-8054-2696-0

Published by B&H Publishing Group,
Nashville, Tennessee

Dewey Decimal Classification: 248.84
Subject Heading: CHRISTIAN LIFE

1 2 3 4 5 6 7 8 9 10   10 09 08 07

Dedication

To Dave and Lynnette Hoy

True friends are a gift from God.

ACKNOWLEDGMENTS

This book was written in the middle of a major life transition, and I have relied heavily on my family and my friends during this chapter of my personal journey. I am grateful to many people. I owe a great debt of thanks to Ted and Lois Griffin. Without their initial encouragement, I doubt this book would ever have been written. My heartfelt thanks to Len Goss, Kim Overcash, Mary Beth Shaw, and the whole team at B&H Publishing Group. My brother Alan offered the use of his cabin in Mississippi for as long as we needed it. I first shared Elijah's story with a receptive audience at Gull Lake Conference Center in Michigan. Colin Smith helped me out at a crucial moment when I needed clarity. I have learned much from the many lunches John Armstrong and I have shared together. Wilbur Ellsworth repeatedly shared his wisdom with me. Brian Bill and Phil Newton have always been there when I needed them. Erwin Lutzer asked me on more than one occasion, "What book are you working on now?" My wife Marlene constantly encouraged me as the manuscript neared completion. Josh, Mark, and Nick keep me going and give me hope for the future. And it is a special joy to welcome Leah and Vanessa to our family.

CONTENTS

INTRODUCTION

The scene is a prep school somewhere in New England. On a beautiful fall morning the bright young men have gathered in English literature class, fearing the worst—long, boring hours arguing about *Beowulf* or the intricacies of iambic pentameter. But lo, it is not to be. Their teacher is brand-new, a graduate who has returned to teach at his alma mater. To him English literature is not about names and rhymes; it's about life—living, dying, loving, caring, feeling. He aims somehow to impart this vision to his young charges.

Suddenly he cries, "Follow me!" and leads the class out into the hallway, down to the glass cases that contain the pictures of former students from long ago. "Look," he says. "Look closely; do you see them?" The pictures are old, cracked, faded, but you can still see their youthful faces. "Look at them carefully. They were once young like you are. They had hopes and dreams just like you do. They had grand ideas too." Then the teacher lowers his voice and says, "Listen, can you hear what they are saying?" The young men press closer to the glass as if to hear the voices of the past come floating up from the cracked and faded pictures. "They're calling out to you. If you listen, you can hear them. They're calling out, '*Carpe diem.*'" These young men don't know Latin, so the phrase is a mystery to them. "*Carpe diem,*" they mumble to one

1

another. "Yes!" he cries out. "That's it. *Carpe diem*. They're saying, '*Carpe diem*.' Can you hear them?" Then he turns to the class egghead, the one with the glasses. "Mr. Stevenson, do you know what *carpe diem* means?" The young man looks puzzled for a moment. Then the meaning comes to him. "Seize the day! *Carpe diem* means, 'seize the day!'" "That's right!" cries the teacher triumphantly. "Seize the day! They are calling out to you from the past—seize the day!"

If you have seen the movie *Dead Poet's Society*, that scene is forever etched in your mind. The past calls to the present—*carpe diem*—"Seize the day!" The future looks to the past and says, *"Carpe diem"*—"Seize the day!" No message is timelier for Christians in the twenty-first century. Either we rise up and seize the day for the glory of God, or we let the moment pass and live to look back with bitter regret over what might have been.

Before we go any further, let me ask a personal question: How much are you willing to risk to become all that God wants you to be? In the spiritual arena what you risk is what you get. Those who risk little, achieve little. Those who risk the most, gain the most. The greatest heroes of the Bible were also the greatest risk-takers for God. That should not surprise us because the life of faith is inherently a life of risk. Go back to the Bible and take a look at the men and women who did great things for God. They were all, without exception, risk-takers. They were people who weren't afraid to lay it all on the line for God.

Most of us know about Noah, the preacher who built an ark. We know about Abraham, who set out for regions unknown because God had promised to show him a better land. We've all heard about Moses, who at the age of eighty led the children of Israel out of Egypt. And we know Joshua and the walls of Jericho, David and Goliath, and Daniel and the lions' den. This book is about a hero whose name you recognize but whose story you may not know. His name is Elijah. He steps onto the stage of biblical history at a low ebb in the history of Israel. When the nation was almost completely given over to idolatry, God raised up a mountain man to confront the evil men who controlled the government of the nation. Jeannette Clift George summarizes his impact this way: "He took on the prophets of Baal and won the contest on Mount Carmel. He, in the name of sovereign God, humbled the posture of a nation's idol worship, brought fire from sodden wood, rain from dry-eyed heaven, and recognition of Jehovah from pagan lips."[1]

He was a little rough around the edges. Make that a lot rough around the edges.

He did things that most people would find peculiar.

He apparently had no fear, except when he got discouraged, and then he ran away.

He could be gentle to a widow and tough as nails with the false prophets.

He was far from perfect.

Sometimes he got discouraged and did foolish things.

Sometimes he gave in to self-pity.

But when he was on his game, which was most of the time, he was awesome.

I don't think Elijah was the easiest man to be around. Feared by kings and false prophets, cheered and beloved by the young men he trained, he was the talk of the nation. He would suddenly appear, deliver a message from God, and then seemingly vanish into thin air for months at a time. He exploded onto the scene, grabbed center stage, came and went as he pleased, riled up the king and his evil wife, and called down fire from heaven. First he humiliated the false prophets, then he slaughtered them. And in the wake of his greatest victory, he ran away and prayed that God would take his life.

What a complicated man he was. I love Elijah because he's a real man. Say what you want, but no one ever called him a plaster saint. Nothing fake about him. At least with Elijah, you never had to wonder what he was thinking or feeling. He wore his heart on his sleeve and captivated a nation. When God needed a man to "seize the day," he called on Elijah, and his mountain man answered the call.

He was a big risk taker for God.

He wasn't afraid to look foolish in the eyes of his countrymen.

His best moments are the stuff of legend, especially the showdown with the prophets of Baal on Mount Carmel. One man versus 850 bad guys. And Elijah, with God's help, beat them all!

Are you ready for some excitement?

Are you tired of the status quo?

Are you ready to seize the day?

As you read this book, ask God to pull you out of your comfort zone. As we journey through the amazing life and times of a man who lived twenty-eight hundred years ago, we'll discover that Elijah speaks today. The voice of God's mountain man echoes across the centuries and says to the twenty-first century, "*Carpe diem*. Seize the day!" As we study Elijah, we'll be changed for the better. And in the end, we'll become more like Jesus. But that's getting ahead of ourselves. Let's enter a time machine and go back twenty-seven centuries to a nation called Israel on the eastern shore of the Mediterranean Sea, to the palace of a man named Ahab. He doesn't know what's about to hit him.

Enter Elijah, God's mountain man who is about to seize the day for God.

Chapter 1

𝒢OD'S MOUNTAIN MAN

"These are times in which a genius would wish to live. It is not in the still calm of life, or the repose of a pacific station, that great characters are formed. The habits of a vigorous mind are formed in contending with difficulties."

ABIGAIL ADAMS

𝑅ight after the tsunami disaster in December 2004, my friend Ramesh Richard, a professor at Dallas Seminary, sent an e-mail that contained a simple, one-sentence prayer. He called it a "dangerous" prayer. The moment I saw that prayer, I knew that it was going to be my prayer for the next chapter of my life. It goes like this: "Lord, do things we're not used to."

Simple.

Concise.

Definitely dangerous.

I started praying that for myself and for my family; and on the first Sunday of January, I told my congregation that we were going to make this our prayer for the new year: "Lord, do things we're not used to." It scared some people to death, and I have discovered that if you pray that prayer, you'd better get ready because God is going to shake you up and shake your family up. And he certainly has done that for my family.

Until recently I have lived in large cities my entire career. After graduating from seminary, I pastored a church in Los Angeles for five years. Then I moved to Dallas where I lived for six more years. Then I moved to a Chicago suburb called Oak Park where I pastored a church for sixteen years. Even though I grew up in a small town, I've lived in big cities all of my adult life. I understand city life; I'm used to the rhythm, the noise, the crowds, the congestion on the freeways, the endless stream of people, the sounds of sirens at night, and the rush of multitudes on their way to work on Monday morning. And I know something about how folks in the city can sometimes be rude to one another, and impatient, and pushy, and not always friendly to newcomers. I learned to love the big city with its endless stream of people, the ethnic neighborhoods, the street festivals, the music, the lights, and all the rest of the action that draws young people away from the farms and the small towns, hoping to make it in the big city, hustling to find their place, eager to start a new life, tired of the slow pace of the hometown where they grew up, and so they move to Miami or Denver or Atlanta or Cleveland or New York or San Francisco or Houston or St. Louis.

Big cities are fun and exciting places to live. I know. I've been there for the last twenty-six years. But all that has suddenly changed in answer to that "dangerous" prayer.

I am writing these words from a cabin overlooking a lake. You get to the cabin by going through a cattle gate and driving a quarter-mile down a gravel road. To get to the gravel road, you take a winding country road that connects to another country road that connects to the Natchez Trace. If you travel nine miles south, you come to the town of Tupelo, Mississippi. You would never get to the cabin by accident. You can hardly get here on purpose. This morning as I look out on the lake, the water is perfectly still. The nearest home is about a half mile away. The lake and the cabin sit on a hundred wooded acres. Two days ago I met a young man driving a pickup truck on the gravel road. He told me that he had been bow-hunting deer, that the field on the other side of the lake was "full of deer," and that the woods were full of wild turkeys. I knew then that I wasn't in Oak Park anymore. You may remember that line from *Green Acres*, the one that goes "Good-bye city life." That pretty much describes our current situation.

We are here because the Lord has called us to be here, at least for the time being. We are here by God's direction, to seek his face so that we may know him better and find out what he wants us to do next. We are certain that this is part of God's answer to the prayer, "Lord, do things we aren't used to." I've discovered that if you pray that way, you'd better buckle your seat belt because God will shake things up. He's not a God of the status quo. First he shakes us up, and then he uses us to shake our world. That's always been God's method. When God wanted to change the world, he told Noah to do something he had never done before (build an ark) to prepare for something he'd never seen before (a flood). When God wanted to bring forth a great nation, he called a successful, middle-aged businessman named Abram and told him to leave Ur of the Chaldees. When God wanted to deliver his people, he found a man slow of speech named Moses and sent him to talk to the pharaoh. When the Lord needed someone to hide the spies in Jericho, he found a prostitute named

Rahab. When God needed someone to defeat Goliath, he chose a shepherd boy named David. When God wanted to deliver his people from destruction, he chose a young girl named Esther. When Christ wanted some men in his inner circle, he chose fishermen and tax collectors, a loudmouth named Peter and two brothers called the "sons of thunder," and told them to drop everything and follow him. Talk about doing things you're not used to. I repeat: He's not a God of the status quo.

"Everyone wants progress. No one wants change." So said a wise friend of mine a few days ago. He was talking about churches and how they say they want to make progress in reaching the world, but no one wants things to change.

Change propels us out of our comfort zone.

Change forces us out of our ruts.

Change destabilizes our routine.

Change challenges our priorities.

Change disrupts our plans.

Change causes us to ask new questions and seek new answers to old questions.

Change introduces us to a whole new set of problems.

Change opens the door to exciting opportunities.

Change stretches us in ways we don't want to be stretched.

Change upsets the apple cart.

Change kicks us out of the recliner.

Change rearranges our daily schedule.

Change is generally a good thing, but it often doesn't seem that way when we're facing it, or just starting to go through it, or trying to find a new comfort zone. Sometimes you end up looking around and saying, "How did we end up here?" And when you ask that question, it's a good thing not to force yourself to answer it quickly.

One writer describes the process of change this way: "It's not so much that we're afraid of change, or so in love with old ways, but it's that place in between we fear . . . it's like being in between trapezes. It's Linus when his blanket is in the dryer. There's nothing to hold on to."[1]

Between trapezes. That's an apt metaphor. There are moments when life suddenly turns into a big game of fruit basket turnover. Suddenly all the familiar landmarks disappear, and you find yourself floating through the air (not necessarily with the greatest of ease), reaching out for something to hold on to. When you look down, you realize that either there isn't a net there or you can't see it. One year ago I was still living in Oak Park, our oldest son Josh had just come home from China, our youngest son Nick was in China, and our middle son Mark was about to go to China. Marlene was going through her breast cancer treatments, I was still pastoring a church, and Josh had not even started dating Leah. Now we're living in a cabin in Mississippi, Marlene's health is much better, Josh is married to Leah, Mark is returning to China for a second year, Nick is studying Chinese, and I'm traveling and speaking around the country. We're learning to trust God in new ways all the time. Marlene continues to gain strength, and we don't have a clue about where we'll be in six months. That's above my pay grade.

There are moments in life when we desperately need a change, but we don't realize it.

Not long ago I was watching a certain speaker on TV when he uttered words that seem profoundly true to me: "If you want what you've never had, you've got to do what you've never done." Most of us know that insanity is doing the same thing over and over again and hoping for different results. Sometimes God looks down from heaven and says, "It's time for a change." There are moments in history when the God of mercy and grace decides that things have gone far enough. Usually God's strategy for judgment is simple. He withdraws his hand of favor and lets us do things on our own for a while. The result is always the same.

We foul it up. Big time.

And God says, "You've gone far enough down that road. It's time for me to intervene." It's precisely at this point that we need to do some careful thinking. Often we have the wrong idea of God's judgment. What is the judgment of God when men turn away from him? God gives them up to their own devices. He lets them follow their own desires. He doesn't try to stop their meteoric descent into the abyss. God abandons the human race by letting men reap what they sow. Nothing more terrible could ever be contemplated. When men "abandon" God in their thinking, God "abandons" them. Why? Because God is a perfect gentleman; he respects the choices we make. If a man or a woman decides to live without him, he says, "Fine. You can live without me. In the end you'll be sorry. But if that's your decision, I'll respect it."

"I Gave It Up Because It Can Kill You"

But there is a deeper reason at work. *God abandons men so that they will see what life is like without God!* In that sense a redemptive purpose stands behind the wrath of God. By letting mankind go their own way, he is not only punishing them. He is also allowing them to see the emptiness of life without him. Recently someone gave me a cartoon that graphically illustrates how this process works. The first frame shows a man saying, "I used to smoke to ease the pain . . . but I gave it up because it can kill you." Then he says, "So I started to drink to ease the pain

. . . but I gave it up because it can kill you." Next frame: "So I started on drugs to ease the pain . . . but I gave it up because it can kill you." Next frame: "So then I had nothing to ease the pain. So I faced the pain . . . and worked through the pain. . . . Now I am pain-free." Final frame, the man stands with his arms outstretched: "What do I do to ease the emptiness?" That's Romans 1 in a nutshell. Turning away from God brings only more pain. But when you get rid of the pain, what do you do about the emptiness? Where does modern man go to solve the deep void within?

Only when a man comes to the end of himself is he ready to think about Jesus Christ. But when that moment of emptiness comes, when he finally faces the God-shaped vacuum inside, when he discovers that disobedience only leads to pain, when he reaps the bitter harvest of his own sin, then and only then has he become a candidate for the grace of God! Unfortunately, some people never figure it out in time. They die without realizing the folly of their own behavior. But others come to the end and finally, after many mistakes, they begin to look up. When they do, they find that God is there waiting for them.

This is the story of one of the greatest men of the Old Testament. He was a prophet, and he was a mountain man who came out of nowhere to step onto center stage. He lived by a brook in a ravine and then in a widow's house. He defeated the prophets of Baal on Mount Carmel and then ran and hid in a cave. He was uncouth and unrefined, yet God used him to shake a nation. Because he didn't follow the status quo, he made everyone around him uncomfortable. And we're still talking about him twenty-eight hundred years later. His name was Elijah. He was God's mountain man.

Seven Evil Kings

In order to understand Elijah, we've got to roll the tape back a few generations before he stepped onto the stage of biblical history. Our journey begins in 1 Kings 15. For most of us this is part of the white pages of the Bible. That is to say, it's a section of the Bible we normally don't look at very much unless we're trying to read through the Bible in a year. That's a shame because these chapters contain enormous spiritual truth that we need to learn. The author of 1 Kings traces the story of the kings of Israel and the kings of Judah, and by putting them up against each other, he draws attention to those who walked with God and those who didn't. For our purposes, we will concentrate on the kings of Israel, the name given to the northern ten tribes after the nation split in 931 BC. The northern ten tribes are usually called *Israel*; the southern two tribes are usually called *Judah*. I call your attention to a succession of kings in the northern ten tribes.

The first king of the northern ten tribes was a man by the name of Jeroboam. We know he was not a good king because he erected images of two golden calves, one at Dan in the north and one at Bethel in the south. And he said to his people, "These are your gods. You do not have to go down to Jerusalem to worship. Go to Dan in the north or to Bethel in the south and there offer your sacrifices to the true god of your nation" (see 1 Kings 12:28–30). And so Jeroboam introduced idolatry into the nation, and he brought down upon his people the wrath of the Lord God.

Jeroboam was succeeded on the throne by his son Nadab. We pick up the story in 1 Kings 15:25–26: "Nadab the son of Jeroboam began to reign over Israel in the second year of Asa king of Judah, and he reigned over Israel two years. He did what was evil in the sight of the LORD and walked in the way of his father, and in his sin which he made Israel to sin." Nadab reigned for only two years because he was assassinated. "In the third year of Asa king of Judah, Baasha the son of Ahijah began to reign over all Israel at Tirzah, and he reigned twenty-four years. He did what was evil in the sight of the LORD and walked in the way of Jeroboam and in his sin which he made Israel to sin" (1 Kings 15:33–34).

So now we have three kings in Israel, each one worse than the one before:

Jeroboam

Nadab

Baasha

Baasha had a son whose name was Elah. "In the twenty-sixth year of Asa king of Judah, Elah the son of Baasha began to reign over Israel in Tirzah, and he reigned two years" (1 Kings 16:8). Verse 13 mentions that "all the sins of Baasha and the sins of Elah his son, which they sinned and which they made Israel to sin, provoking the LORD God of Israel to anger with their idols." Here's the fourth king, and he's as bad as the first three. After two years a man named Zimri assassinates Elah. First Kings 16:15 says Zimri reigned only seven days. That's hardly long enough to begin the makeover of the palace. You hardly have time to move out the old furniture and move in the new. After one week on the throne, he was assassinated by a man named Omri "because of the sins he had committed, doing evil in the eyes of the LORD, and walking in the ways of Jeroboam and the sin he had committed and caused Israel to commit" (1 Kings 16:19 NIV).

So here's the list of kings so far:

Jeroboam

Nadab

Baasha

Elah

Zimri

Omri

Omri was the worst of all. Look at 1 Kings 16:25: "Omri did what was evil in the sight of the LORD, and did more evil than all who were before him."

There is yet one more name in this long list of the evil kings of Israel, a name you will recognize. We are told in 1 Kings 16:28 that "Omri slept with his fathers and was buried in Samaria, and Ahab his son reigned in his place." You've heard that name. These other fellows we don't know much about, but Ahab we know. You've heard of him, and you've probably heard of his wife Jezebel.

At last we come to the bottom line.

"Ahab the son of Omri did evil in the sight of the LORD, more than all who were before him. And as if it had been a light thing for him to walk in the sins of Jeroboam the son of Nebat, he took for his wife Jezebel the daughter of Ethbaal king of the Sidonians, and went and served Baal and worshiped him. He erected an altar for Baal in the house of Baal, which he built in Samaria. And Ahab made an Asherah. Ahab did more to provoke the LORD, the God of Israel, to anger than all the kings of Israel who were before him" (1 Kings 16:30–33).

So the story unfolds this way:

Jeroboam did evil in the eyes of the Lord.

Nadab his son did evil in the eyes of the Lord.

He was assassinated by Baasha who did evil in the eyes of the Lord.

He was followed by his son Elah who did evil in the eyes of the Lord.

He was assassinated by Zimri who did evil in the eyes of the Lord.

He was assassinated by Omri who did even more evil in the eyes of the Lord.

He was succeeded by his son Ahab who was the worst of all the kings of Israel to this point.

From Jeroboam to Nadab to Baasha to Elah to Zimri to Omri to Ahab, we are not going up. The nation is spiraling downward, and it seems that just when you think things can't get any worse, the bottom falls out, and the nation descends even further into idolatry and immorality.

"God Gave Them Up"

As I read this sordid story of evil men who misled their own people, I ask myself a question: Where is God? We are told that what these men did provoked the Lord. If so, where was he? I submit to you that for many years he was nowhere to be found. Sometimes God judges us by actively intervening, and sometimes God judges a people and a nation simply by leaving them alone. Romans 1 explains this process in great detail. If you want to understand the flow of history and the reason great nations decline, if you want to know why every human empire eventually implodes, read Romans 1. Because men suppress the truth about God, they turn to idolatry. Because they forsake God, he forsakes them. Three times in Romans 1 Paul uses a phrase that describes God's response to human rebellion:

> "God gave them up" (v. 24).
> "God gave them up" (v. 26).
> "God gave them up" (v. 28).

Other translations use a phrase like "*God gave them over.*" It comes from a Greek word that means to hand over in judgment. It's what happens at the end of the trial when the judge says to the

bailiff, "Take this man away." He is "handed over" for imprison-
ment. That's what is happening in Romans 1. When any nation
says, "*Lord, we don't need you,*" God says, "Fine; have it your way."
C. S. Lewis said that there are really only two prayers we can pray.
Every prayer in the universe falls into one of two categories:

"Your will be done," or

"My will be done."

If we say to God, "I do not want to do your will; my will be
done," God says, "Have it your way, but you won't be happy with
the results." All of us know people who are living illustrations
of this principle. You may say, "I've got a husband . . . ," or "I've
got a wife . . . ," or "I've got a child . . . ," or "I've got a friend for
whom that process of God's judgment is taking place in their
life." When they hurdle headlong away from the Lord, God
doesn't have to do anything to judge them; they judge themselves
by their own rebellion.

The Frog in the Kettle

I was interviewed by a man who works for a pro-family organization in Wisconsin. He wanted to talk to me because he knew
that Oak Park is heavily influenced by the homosexual community. We were the first community in Illinois to pass a non-
discrimination ordinance protecting gays and lesbians. We were
the first community in the Midwest to elect a lesbian as a village
president. We were one of the first communities in the nation
with a registry for domestic partners. I think it's fair to say that
the homosexual community in Oak Park is strong. In September
2004, Calvary Memorial Church got quite a bit of publicity in
Chicago because I preached for five weeks about marriage and

the family from God's point of view.[2] One Sunday I preached on "The Truth about Same-Sex Marriage." We were picketed by three different gay rights groups, and the Chicago media covered it extensively. *Leadership Journal* wrote an article about it.[3] I won't say much about that except to say that what the devil meant for evil, God meant for good. We discovered that once you get past all the picketers and all the protesters, God used our church's willingness to take a stand to open doors for communication. God gave us amazing opportunities to talk to people inside the gay community and to show them the love of Jesus Christ.

When the man from Wisconsin called me, he wanted to know what our church was doing in this area. Then he said to me, "What your church did is unusual. Most evangelical churches these days are unwilling to tackle those issues. Why do you think that is?" There are lots of answers to that question, but if you go underneath the surface, I think too many pastors and too many elder boards are just plain scared. I think we're just scared of what will happen in the community. I think we're scared of bad publicity. I think we're scared of the kind of thing that happened in Oak Park. And sometimes we're scared of what people inside the church will say. I discovered that when I preached about it, I wasn't the most popular person in my own congregation. I didn't have 100-percent support from my own people. Inside the evangelical church there is a growing softness on the issue of homosexuality largely because so many families inside our own churches have sons and daughters and friends and ex-wives and ex-husbands who have gone into that way of life. But that's not the only problem. You can hardly find a sitcom on TV that doesn't have an obligatory friendly, nice, normal gay character on it. We're being fed a constant diet of pro-homosexual propaganda from Hollywood. And say what we will, we aren't telling the truth if we claim that we're not impacted by that. Billy Graham commented that one of the problems inside the church is that today we laugh at things that used to embarrass us thirty or forty years ago. Or even worse, we don't even laugh anymore. We've become like the proverbial frog in the kettle. When you put a frog in a kettle of cold water and slowly heat it up, the frog's body adjusts to the temperature so that it doesn't notice that the water is becoming dangerously hot. Finally the water boils the frog because it has become used to that which eventually kills it. Something like that has happened to us as the culture has slowly changed around us. We've gotten used to the gradual moral decline so that things that used to seem evil to us don't seem so bad nowadays. As things have declined morally and spiritually in the culture around us, the church has subtly changed along with the culture. I'm not saying we've changed our convictions, but we are less willing to go out on a limb for what the Bible really says than we were a generation or two ago. I think it's high time we regained some backbone inside the evangelical church.

Hot Button Issues

The July 11, 2005 issue of *Time* magazine contained an article by Daniel Eisenberg in which he talked about six hot button issues that are at stake in the battle over the Supreme Court. His list includes abortion and gay rights, church and state, crime, affirmative action, state's rights, and the right to die.[4] I think Mr. Eisenberg is absolutely right when he uses the term *hot button issues* because there is a moral and spiritual component to every one of them. We live in the midst of a cultural and spiritual battle that is being waged on many fronts. After the terrorists attacked the London subways, British Prime Minister Tony Blair said that people who blow up buildings and blow themselves up in London subways are following an "evil ideology." He is right. Leadership is about more than politics and winning elections. And it's about much more than whose agenda will prevail. Every decision has a moral component because every decision comes from a worldview that either leads us to God or away from God. And that brings us back to those evil kings of Israel. Jeroboam did evil. Nadab did evil. Baasha did evil. Elah did evil. Zimri did evil. Omri was worse than the first five, and his son Ahab was the worst of all.

Do you know what Ahab did? According to 1 Kings 16, in the days of Ahab, it became trivial to offer sacrifices to idols. The people of God just didn't care anymore. Is that not the Old Testament version of Romans 1? And what is the end of Romans 1? When men turn away from God, God gives them over to face the consequences of their own evil choices. Romans 1:24–32 contains a long list of sins that includes homosexuality, but it is far more than that. Romans 1 pictures the total disintegration of society as it turns away from God. The final step is that evil is not only tolerated; it is celebrated (v. 32).

How is that so different from America in the twenty-first century? Hear the Word of the Lord:

"Blessed is the nation whose God is the LORD"
(Ps. 33:12).

"Righteousness exalts a nation, but sin is a reproach to any people" (Prov. 14:34).

"Those who forsake the law praise the wicked, but those who keep the law strive against them" (Prov. 28:4).

"When the righteous triumph, there is great glory, but when the wicked rise, people hide themselves" (Prov. 28:12).

"When the wicked rise, people hide themselves, but when they perish, the righteous increase" (Prov. 28:28).

"When the righteous increase, the people rejoice, but when the wicked rule, the people groan" (Prov. 29:2).

"When the wicked increase, transgression increases, but the righteous will look upon their downfall" (Prov. 29:16).

Here's one more verse. I actually laughed when I found this one. Solomon's wisdom cheered me up. Proverbs 11:10 declares that "when it goes well with the righteous, the city rejoices, and when the wicked perish there are shouts of gladness."

How bad can it get?

Jeroboam to Nadab.

Nadab to Baasha.

Baasha to Elah.

Elah to Zimri.

Zimri to Omri.

Omri to Ahab.

Ahab was the worst of all, and Jezebel was his evil wife.

And . . . Bam!

That brings me at last to the end of 1 Kings 16 and the beginning of 1 Kings 17. In the NIV, verse 1 begins with the word "now." In the Hebrew it's literally "and." That's important because the author wants us to catch the flow of history from God's point of view. It's "and," not simply "now." Let's go over that list one more time. Here are the seven evil kings of Israel from 1 Kings 15–16:

Jeroboam

Nadab

Baasha

Elah

Zimri

Omri

Ahab

Now we're down in the sewer. The nation is far gone in immorality and idolatry. Things appear to be totally hopeless. Note the little word *and*. Something is about to happen.

God is about to enter the situation.

God's about to interject himself.

Almighty God is about to be heard.

When times are bad and the situation is hopeless, God has a man. "Now Elijah the Tishbite, from Tishbe in Gilead, said to Ahab" (1 Kings 17:1 NIV). Have you ever watched Emeril Lagasse on the Food Network? If you've seen him, you know what he does when he is preparing a recipe on camera. There's something he says when he's about to add some cinnamon or some salt or some garlic to the mixture. He'll pour it on, and then he'll shout, "Bam!"

A little cinnamon. Bam!

A little salt. Bam!

A little garlic. Bam!

That's what's happening here. "And Elijah . . . said to Ahab." Bam! The prophet of God shows up. No preparation. No warning. No genealogy at all. In some Jewish traditions, not mainline Judaism, but in some Jewish traditions they even think Elijah was an angel because like Melchizedek he comes out of nowhere. We don't know anything about his parents or grandparents. The Jews loved genealogy, but nothing is recorded about his background.

Let's do the list again:

Jeroboam

Nadab

Baasha

Elah

Zimri

Omri

Ahab

Elijah. Bam! Now they've heard from God. No wonder they thought he was an angel, though that was not what Ahab thought. When times are bad and the situation is hopeless, God has a man whose name is Elijah. Alexander Whyte called him "a Mount Sinai of a man with a heart like a thunderstorm." F. B. Meyer called him a "colossus among men." Alexander McClaren called him "the Martin Luther of the Old Testament." Oswald Sanders says, "Elijah appeared at zero hour in Israel's history. . . . Like a meteor, he flashed across the inky blackness of Israel's spiritual night."[5]

Before we go any further, here are a few facts about Elijah:

1. *He was one of the greatest prophets in the Old Testament.* You could easily argue that Moses was the greatest prophet, but he was also a leader of his people. If you want to talk about a pure prophet who wasn't involved in running the government, it's hard

to argue against Elijah as the greatest. He comes at the head of the class.

2. *Though he lived almost three thousand years ago, he speaks to us with amazing contemporary power.* His message speaks to at least five different groups of people.

He speaks to those who have a hard lot in life.

He speaks to those who feel alone in the world.

He speaks to those who feel their life has produced few results.

He speaks to those who feel helpless against the tide of evil.

He speaks to those who have failed, which includes, I suppose, all of us at one time or another.

3. *We know almost nothing about his background.* He's a Tishbite, which means he's from Tishbe in Gilead. To this day no one has ever found a village or a town named Tishbe. That simply means it was a small village up in the mountains. Gilead we know, and that's important. Gilead was on the eastern side of the Jordan River. It would be in modern-day Jordan, across the Jordan River from the city of Jericho. In fact, if you ever go to Jericho, look to the east and you will see the mountains of Gilead. That's really the only clue we have about this man.

Elijah was a mountain man. Because he came from the mountains, he was probably a bit uncouth. Because he came from the mountains, he wasn't very refined. Because he came from the mountains, he wouldn't have had the same level of education as those who were raised in the city of Jerusalem. In that day people from the city tended to look down their noses at men from the mountains the same way people today sometimes look down at folks who come from the hills. Hill people. Hillbillies. Elijah was like an Old Testament hillbilly. Before you laugh too much, remember this. You don't want to make those people mad. You'll lose that argument. You might lose something else too. You don't want to mess with mountain folks. They're a tough breed.

"The Lord Is My God"

Let's do it again to just make sure we've got the picture:

Jeroboam

Nadab

Baasha

Elah

Zimri

Omri

Ahab

They're so far down in the pit, a city boy isn't up for that kind of job. God didn't want a seminary graduate. God didn't want anybody too refined. God wanted somebody cut from rough cloth, somebody who didn't mind wearing burlap, somebody with calloused hands, somebody whose nouns and verbs might not always agree. God wanted a man raised in the mountains who was not scared of wicked King Ahab, that evil toad squatting on the throne of Israel. When God wanted a man to go up against that evil king and his evil wife, he had to go to the mountains to find him.

When he did, he got a man. He didn't get a boy. He got a man, and he sent that man to see the king. Elijah's name tells us about his character. *El* is God, and *Jah* is like Jehovah or Yahweh. The *i* in Elijah means *my*. Literally Elijah's name means "the Lord is my God." "Hello. My name's Ray. What's your name?" "My name is *The Lord is my God*." Any questions? "Hello, Ahab. Hello, Jezebel. My name is *The Lord is my God*."

Ahab was not laughing. He didn't see anything funny about that. You can imagine the color draining out of his face as this uncouth man from the mountains strides into his presence with a message from the Lord God in heaven. Oh, we need men like that today. Elijah was a troublemaker for the Lord. He was called to serve in a day of moral apostasy.

James 5:17 adds one fascinating fact about Elijah when it calls him a man "with a nature like ours." The King James says he was a man of "like passions." He was like you, and he was like me. Read the story and see for yourself. Elijah had his ups and downs. He was a little rough around the edges. Not so polished. Not so refined. You're not going to have Elijah over to watch the World Series because you don't know when he's going to go off. He's that kind of man. When he gets a message from God, he's going to take action. You're not going to talk him out of it either. As we will see, he was far from perfect. He's got a temper, and he is prone to depression and discouragement. James used him as an example for us to follow because, despite his human weaknesses, he was a man of prayer who walked with God in the midst of an evil generation. Though he was an imperfect mountain man, he was also a man of prayer and enormous faith in God. And that's why he's in the Bible.

Elijah's Secret

Consider what he said to Ahab: "As the LORD the God of Israel lives, before whom I stand, there shall be neither dew nor rain these years, except by my word" (1 Kings 17:1). What was his secret? What made him tick? The answer is right here.

First, he believed in the living God. "Ahab, my God is alive. What about yours? You worship Baal, who lives during the wet season and dies during the dry season. I serve the living God. I believe in the living God."

Second, he served the covenant God. He called him "the God of Israel."

Third, he lived in the presence of God. "The God . . . before whom I stand." Proverbs says the fear of the Lord brings safety. When Elijah stood before Ahab, he was not afraid because Elijah said, "I stand before Almighty God. Ahab, you are nothing to me." One reason we are not bolder and more courageous is because we have more respect for men than we do for Almighty God. The fear of man brings a snare, but he who trusts in the Lord will be kept safe (see Prov. 29:25). So that is no small thing when Elijah says, "I stand in the presence of God." As far as he was concerned, Ahab didn't even matter. All he did was show up and deliver God's message.

Fourth, he obeyed the call of God. "There shall be neither dew nor rain these years, except by my word." What does that mean? Ahab worshipped Baal, and Baal was the god of fertility. The Canaanites believed Baal appeared in the thunderclouds and the rainstorms. They set up their altars on mountaintops so they could be closer to their god. When people came to worship Baal, they encountered the men and women who served in the priesthood. There were two parts of the religion of Baal—illicit sex and child sacrifice. If you were praying for rain, you would offer your sacrifice, and then you would have a sexual encounter with a priest or a priestess of Baal. They believed that somehow the sexual act joined them with Baal, the god of fertility. And if things were really bad, you would bring your children and offer them to Baal. It was a religion of perverted sex and child sacrifice in the name of personal peace and affluence. Does that sound familiar? Nothing in three thousand years has really changed.

A Radical Man

Elijah's life is the story of a truly radical man. The word *radical* is from the Latin word *radix*, meaning "root." So many of us live in the clouds, and we wonder why we have no courage. Elijah was a man who got down to the root of things. You know what a radical Christian is? A radical Christian is nothing more than somebody who's gotten down to the root issues of life and figured out what matters and what doesn't matter. And Elijah had figured it out.

Our young people have figured this out better than people my age. I think Christian young people of the up-and-coming generation are much more radically oriented for Jesus than we are. We need to catch up with the next generation. They have figured out that this world is plastic and if you follow the ways of this world you are going to be empty at the end. God bless those radical young Christians who have gone down to the root issues of life.

Elijah was a radical man.

We could use a few more like him today.

When Elisha saw Elijah go up into heaven, he cried out, "Where is the Lord God of Elijah?"

Here is the question for today: "Where are the Elijahs of the Lord God?"

Chapter 2

ᗅRY BROOK UNIVERSITY

"Conversation enriches the understanding,
but solitude is the school of genius."
RALPH WALDO EMERSON

Several generations ago British Bible teacher F. B. Meyer wrote a short book called *Elijah and the Secret of His Power.* In his introduction he noted that some people may think it rash to study Elijah's life because he was such a great man that we can never hope to be like him. We may admire him, but we also acknowledge that he belongs to a different and higher category than ordinary mortals. Meyer offered this reply: "Some of my readers may be disposed to charge me with rashness in attempting to delineate the life of Elijah—this Colossus among ordinary men, who dwarfs us while his own noble proportions defy the belittling perspective of long distance. But my excuse will be found in the thought, reiterated on many a succeeding page, that the life of this mighty man was wrought out through the indwelling of that Holy Spirit, which is equally within reach of those who will believe and obey."[1]

Then he offers this additional thought, which I believe to be 100-percent correct: "There is nothing the Church of today needs so much as spiritual power; and there is nothing which we can have so easily, if only we are prepared to pay the price."[2] That's an unusual sentence if you think about it. We may "easily" have spiritual power if we are willing to "pay the price." It sounds at first glance like a contradiction in terms, and perhaps it is, until you probe deeper. *God's blessings are freely given but only to those who want them badly.* God does not dispense his power to those who do not want it or to those who are only playing games. If Elijah's life teaches us anything, it is that God delights to use unlikely men whose hearts are fully his.

A Journey, Not a Destination

In recent years I have come to think of the spiritual life as a journey and not as a destination. *No one ever fully "arrives" in this life.* We all press forward, forgetting those things that are behind and pressing on to the mark of the high calling of God in Christ Jesus. Even Paul said, "I have not yet attained" (cf. Phil. 3:12–13). Elijah's life, with its thrilling highs and discouraging lows, with its unexpected twists and turns, teaches us that God is infinitely creative in the ways he deals with his children. Let this be our motto as we journey onward: *Expect the unexpected.* In that sense, Meyer is exactly right. "Paying the price" means (among other things) following God wherever he leads us, knowing that the road ahead is not likely to be what we thought it would be. That's why the prayer, "Lord, do things I'm not used to," is so powerful. It moves us out of the status quo and puts us in a place where we are ready to expect the unexpected. I received an e-mail from a friend who has built a fine career for himself in his chosen field. He has a happy marriage, a wonderful family, a nice house, a good reputation, and an effective ministry in his local church. By all outward appearances he is doing exactly what God wants him to do. He wrote to say that he and his wife will be attending a conference soon that "gathers folks from all over the world who are involved in missions, and we are going to see if God might have something different for us for the next ten years or so." Then he added this phrase: "Sound familiar?" As a matter of fact, it sounds very familiar, and I know lots of people in their midlife years who are asking, "Lord, how can I be most effective for you with the years that are left to me?" God bless my friend, and God bless all those Spirit-led risk takers who have the courage at least to ask the right questions.

Elijah would understand. *He knew instinctively that following God meant moving out of his comfort zone.* In his case it meant confronting an evil king and speaking truth to power. But what he didn't know is that following God would lead him from the king's palace into months and perhaps years of obscurity, hiding by a brook. And that's where we rejoin Elijah's journey.

A Sudden Change of Direction

As we saw in the last chapter, Elijah's story began with seven wicked kings of Israel and one mountain man in whose heart God had ignited a kingdom passion. These were the seven wicked kings:

Jeroboam

Nadab

Baasha

Elah

Zimri

Omri

Ahab

Down the spiral went. *Down the people of God went because
their kings were leading them in the wrong direction.* We are told that
Baasha was worse than the ones before, and Omri was worse than
the ones before. When we get to Ahab, we are told that he was the
worst of all because he had married that wicked woman Jezebel
who came from the region of Sidon, in modern-day Lebanon,
north of the land of Israel. She was an out-and-out pagan,
a worshipper of Baal. When Ahab married Jezebel, she brought
her Baal worship directly into the nation of Israel, and under her
influence Ahab built a temple to Baal and promoted idolatry until
it became like nothing for the people to worship Baal.

Into that awful situation God sent his mountain man, Elijah
the Tishbite from the village of Tishbe, an unknown village in
the mountains of Gilead. God sent his mountain man down to a
king named Ahab with a simple message: "As the LORD the God
of Israel lives, before whom I stand, there shall be neither dew
nor rain these years, except by my word" (1 Kings 17:1). Nothing
is said about the king's reaction, mostly because it doesn't really
matter. What matters is that God has interjected himself into a
deteriorating situation, and he does so by means of a mountain
man named Elijah.

If I didn't know anything else about the story, I would expect
that the next sentence would read something like this: "And Elijah

stayed in the palace and spoke again and again to King Ahab until the king came to repentance." Or I would expect the next verse to read, "Elijah began to tear down the temple of Baal." Or possibly, "Elijah went up to the high places and tore down the altars to Baal." Or maybe something like this: "Elijah began to go from village to village, preaching the true God and calling the nation to repentance." But that is not what the next verse reads.

Since Elijah had just come out of the mountains and out of total obscurity, and had been brought by God to stand before the wicked king Ahab, and had declared God's message of coming judgment on the nation, the next verse says what we do not expect, words that must have come as a surprise to Elijah himself. This is what 1 Kings 17:2 actually says: "And the word of the LORD came to him." I imagine this happened while he was standing before Ahab or just as he was leaving his presence.

Elijah now receives further instructions from God. "Depart from here" (v. 3). *Here* being the presence of the king. *Here* being the capital of the northern empire. "Depart from here and turn eastward and hide yourself by the brook Cherith, which is east of the Jordan" (v. 3). When you read of the brook, don't think of a river. The word refers to a wadi, a dry creek bed, which during the wet season would be flowing with water but during the dry season would be dry. The prophet receives further instruction in verse 4: "You shall drink from the brook, and I have commanded the ravens to feed you there." So he did what the Lord told him to do. He went to the Cherith ravine east of the Jordan and stayed there. Verses 6–7 give us the end of the story: "And the ravens brought him bread and meat in the morning, and bread and meat in the evening, and he drank from the brook. And after a while the brook dried up, because there was no rain in the land."

And so we trace the life of Elijah this way. God calls him from the mountains of Gilead to the king's palace. From there he crosses the Jordan River and comes to a ravine by the brook Cherith where he hides himself. There he is to stay until further notice. As I read the story, I ask myself, "Why in the world would the Lord do this?" I think Elijah must have been somewhat disappointed when this word came down from the Lord. It's a bit mystifying if you think about it. First there are those seven evil kings, one after another, dragging the nation into a moral cesspool. Then bam! Elijah steps on the scene. And just as suddenly he disappears. Just as quickly as he comes, just that quickly he is sent into obscurity, silence, and solitude.

A. W. Tozer said, *"It is doubtful that God can use any man greatly until he has hurt him deeply."* Are you willing for God suddenly to redirect your steps, especially if that redirection leads you in a way you did not plan to go? Are you willing to follow the Lord not just through green pastures by still waters, but are you also willing to follow the Lord if the path leads down to a ravine where you must hide yourself?

What lessons should we learn from Elijah's God-directed time by the brook? Let me suggest just a few of them to you.

God's will is revealed to us one step at a time. Not long ago I heard a man say that when God wants to show us his will, he gives us a flashlight, not a road map. We are given just enough light to peer into the darkness and take the next step. Personally I much prefer to have a road map when I set out on a journey. Better yet, I like having a GPS tracker in my car so that I know where I am at every moment. God does have a road map for your life, but he's got the only copy, and it's locked up on the third floor of the administration building in heaven. And he has your life on his heavenly GPS tracker, but he's the only one who can see it. Instead of a map or a GPS tracker, he gives us a flashlight and says, "Trust me and take the next step."

God's instructions to Elijah are clear, precise, and unmistakable. "Elijah, I have called you from the mountains and brought you before the king. You think your public ministry is just beginning, but you have spoken exactly one sentence to the king. Now turn around. Leave this place. Go across the Jordan River. Go to the Cherith ravine and hide yourself there." You can imagine Elijah saying, "Lord, you don't understand. I'm called to speak truth in power. I've got ten or fifteen messages I'm ready to preach. I've barely gotten through the introduction of message number one. Lord, don't you want me to stay here and preach?"

And God says, "No. Your work is done. One sentence was enough for the king. Leave this place. Go and hide yourself in the ravine."

That must have been disappointing or at least a surprising word. We must learn the lesson that Elijah had to learn, that God's will is revealed to us one step at a time.

Here are some questions to ponder. When God told Elijah to go and hide himself in the ravine, did he know how long he was going to be there? No. When God told him to go and hide in the ravine, did he know where he would go next? No. Did he have any inkling of the showdown with the prophets of Baal on Mount Carmel? No. Did he have any idea that one day he would be calling down fire from heaven? No. When God told him to go hide himself in the ravine, did he know that one day he would be carried to heaven in a fiery chariot? No. When God told him to go hide himself in the ravine, what exactly did Elijah know? Elijah knew one thing: he was to go and hide himself in the ravine, and that's all he knew.

If Elijah has any hope of doing all God wants him to do, his first stop must be the ravine by the brook Cherith. You can't get around the ravines of life. You can't bypass that part of your spiritual journey. It's a lot more exciting to be up on the mountain facing down the prophets of Baal and calling down fire from heaven. But if you want to get to the mountaintop, you've got to go by way of the ravine. You've got to spend a few years going to school at DBU, Dry Brook University. You'll never get to Mount Carmel Graduate School without an undergrad degree at DBU.

God's timetable and ours are not the same. Why was it to Elijah's advantage to go and hide himself? For one thing, he had just told the king there would be a drought in the land. But at that moment they had water in their cisterns and food in their storage rooms. It would take quite a few months for the full force of the drought to take effect in the nation. Elijah needed to hide so God could do his work. Second, once the drought began to take hold in Israel, Elijah would be public enemy number one. So hiding Elijah was God's way of protecting him during that time. Third, God wanted to use this drought to expose Baal, who was thought to be the god of fertility. The people believed he was the god who brought the rain that watered their crops. The drought proved that Baal had no real power. The God of Israel is the God of the drought; he is also the God of the rain.

I imagine that life by the creek after the first 150 days or so wasn't really that exciting. They didn't have cable TV in the Cherith ravine. No ESPN. No satellite TV. No Internet hookup. No way to get e-mail. Nobody dropping by for a visit. Elijah got up in the morning, drank some water from the brook, and ate the food the ravens brought. Then he rested. In the evening he drank some more water and ate some more food from the ravens. Talk about a monotonous routine, but this was God's plan for Elijah. His timetable and ours are rarely the same.

I have a friend who after a number of years of successful ministry is not currently serving in a local church. As I write these words, he is in fact unemployed. It happens that his parents are in their nineties and need his help. His mother in particular is in declining health, and his father needs help making wise decisions. He wrote me recently to say that he had spent several weeks with his parents, staying with his father while his mother is in the hospital. At the moment he is searching for an assisted-care living facility where they can both live once his mother is released from the hospital. He commented that he was writing his e-mail on the fly from a coffee shop because his father doesn't like him to be gone from home for any length of time. Years ago I knew his parents because they were well-known Christian leaders. Now the advancing years have taken their toll, and my friend is caring for his parents and at the same time worrying about his own future. He has a few leads but nothing definite.

I wrote him back and said what was on my heart. For years my friend stood in front of people and led in a public way. He had a ministry that impacted his entire region for Christ. Now he is hidden from the world's view. Day after day his horizon is circumscribed by the needs of an aged mother and father. The roles are now reversed. They are children, and he is the parent. They trust him to make wise decisions for them. All of it, plus the weight of his own uncertainty, weighs heavily on him. He did not utter a single complaining word, but I know how difficult it must be. I told him that although the world does not notice what he is doing, it doesn't matter because he is doing the Lord's work just as much as when he got a paycheck and served in a local church. You honor God when you care for your elderly parents. He is doing a noble thing, and God will honor him for it. I have no idea how long my friend will be without a regular job. For the moment he is hidden by the brook just as surely as Elijah was hidden in the ravine. I told him I was praying that he would have wisdom and endurance. But mostly endurance. Wisdom we always need, but endurance is one of those biblical characteristics we don't talk about often. But there are times when what we need is simply the strength to keep on going, especially when God's timetable and ours are not the same.

A century ago the artist John Ruskin penned these beautiful words:

> There is no music in a rest, but there is making of music in it. In our whole life-melody, the music is broken off here and there by "rests," and we foolishly think we have come to the end of time. God sends a time of forced leisure—sickness, disappointed plans, frustrated efforts—and makes a sudden pause in the choral hymn of our lives and we lament that our voices must be silent, and our part missing in the music which ever goes up to the ear of the Creator. How does the musician read the rest? See him beat time with unvarying count and catch up the next note true and steady, as if no breaking place had come between. Not without design does God write the music of our lives. But be it ours to learn the time and not be dismayed at the "rests." They are not to be slurred over, nor to be omitted, nor to destroy the melody, nor to change the keynote. If we look up, God himself will beat time for us.

With the eye on him we shall strike the next note full
and clear.[3]

There are times for all of us when the "music" seems to
stop and we wonder if the melody will ever start again. But like
Elijah in the ravine, we must be patient and wait for the Divine
Conductor to lift his baton and begin the music again.

God's delays teach us to trust him in new ways. Psalm 78
recounts the spiritual experience of the nation of Israel during
their forty years in the Sinai wilderness. When people thought
they were going to starve in the desert, they spoke against God by
asking this question: "Can God spread a table in the wilderness?"
(v. 19). They thought the answer was no, but God sent manna
and quail, and for forty years he set a table in the wilderness.
"Can God set a table in the wilderness?" We all have to come to
the place where we answer that question not just theoretically
but personally. It's one thing for someone to say God will supply
all your needs and he'll take care of you. *You've got to come to the
place where you decide for yourself whether that's true.*

Several of my friends are about to make job changes and
major career moves. In more than one case it means leaving one
area for another part of the country; sometimes it means leaving
a job with no certainty about a future paycheck. Since I've been
in both situations myself, I know how unsettling it can be. Many
years ago my friend Jerry Hansen gave me a piece of advice for
handling moments like this. The human tendency is to look at
change as bad and to value stability above everything else. It's true
that moving to Montana (or wherever) is going to mean an abrupt
change in scenery; and it probably also means you're going to have
to start at ground zero making new friends, finding a new church,
and putting your children in a new school. That's not easy, and it

won't happen overnight. It may take months or even a year or two before you truly feel settled and "at home" again.

When I was between jobs and more or less drifting along in thin air, Jerry took me out to eat one day and told me something like this: "Ray, you need to enjoy this part of your life. If you fight what God is doing, it will just take things longer to work out. But if you relax and let God lead you, eventually you'll look back and see God's hand every step of the way." Then he gave me the punch line: "Don't forget. It doesn't get any better than this." I still smile years later when I think of those words because he was absolutely right. How many hours—days, weeks, months— do we waste fretting over our circumstances and dreaming of better days when all our problems will be behind us? In truth, those "better days" never really come—not perfectly, not in a fallen world where nothing works right all the time. Is there a theological truth behind this? Absolutely. If God is God, then he is just as much the God of your cloudy days as he is the God of bright sunshine. While reading my personal journal, I happened across a quotation I recorded several years ago: "You can't push a river. You've got to let it flow." God's work in your life is like a river flowing steadily toward its appointed destination. Right now your "river" may seem to have taken a detour, and you may feel like trying to rush the current along. It can't be done. The river can't be rushed.

Are you worried about your future? Fear not. Don't rush the river. Enjoy these days as part of God's plan for your life. Go with the flow, and soon enough God will bring you into a safe harbor. Enjoy the blessings of today and remember that everything good comes from your Father in heaven. God's delays teach us to trust him in new ways. And God was doing something in Elijah's life down by the brook Cherith that he didn't fully understand at the time.

God's power works even in our absence. It's easy for us to get an inflated sense of our own importance. I can imagine Elijah saying, *"Lord, you need me. Ahab needs me. The nation needs me. I'm a preacher of your Word. I've just barely gotten started. You let me say one sentence, and then you make me go off to the brook. Lord, you need me to speak to the nation."* As French president Charles de Galle said, the graveyards are filled with indispensable men. Do you want to make God laugh? Tell him your plans. Bob Pierce, the founder of World Vision, said that early on he learned to pray a simple prayer each morning: "Oh Lord, I give you the right to change my agenda anytime you want, and you don't have to inform me in advance." *It is a great advance in the spiritual life when we come to understand that God doesn't need us to do anything.* He speaks and the stars begin to shine. He speaks and a rabbit hops across the forest. He speaks and the birds start to fly and the fish start to swim. He speaks and here we are. He speaks again and we are gone. God's power does not depend on our personal presence. He can work with us; he can work without us.

Many of us struggle with this concept. *God was doing just fine as God before you showed up. He'll do just fine after you are gone.* His power works even in our absence. He was saying to Elijah, "You gave my word. Now go and hide. The power is not in you; the power is in my word." Faith comes by hearing and hearing by the word of God (Rom. 10:17). Elijah must learn that God can work with him or without him. When Martin Luther was asked how he accounted for the epochal changes wrought by the Protestant Reformation, he replied by saying, "I sat in Wittenberg drinking my beer, and the Word did the work." We tend to get hung up on the first part of that statement, but it's not the beer that matters. It could be coffee or tea or milk. It's the Word that does the work. And that work goes on with us or without us.

Several years ago during the annual pastors conference at Moody Bible Institute, Alistair Begg, pastor of the Parkside Church in the Cleveland area, spoke on our need to depend fully on the Lord and not on our own resources. As he came to the close, he told the story of how King Jehoshaphat prayed in 2 Chronicles 20. The Ammonites and the Moabites were moving in a vast army toward Jerusalem. There were so many of them and they were so well armed that the men of Israel would never be able to defeat them. As the invaders came closer and closer, the situation looked increasingly hopeless. The king called for a nationwide fast. Men from every town and village gathered in Jerusalem to seek the Lord. Jehoshaphat stood before them and offered one of the greatest prayers in the Bible (2 Chron. 20:6–12). He begins by declaring God's greatness: "O LORD, God of our fathers, are you not the God who is in heaven? You rule over all the kingdoms of the nations. Power and might are in your hand, and no one can withstand you" (v. 6 NIV). Then he reminds God of the promises he made to take care of his people when they were in trouble. Then he tells God, "We're in big trouble now!" He freely admits, "We have no power to face this vast army that is attacking us" (v. 12 NIV). And he concludes with this simple confession: "We do not know what to do, but our eyes are upon you" (v. 12 NIV). *God's answer came through a prophet who told the people to "stand still and see the salvation of the Lord."* The next day Jehoshaphat put the male singers at the head of the army and sent them out to do battle. They literally stood still and watched as the Lord sent confusion into the enemy ranks. The Moabites and Ammonites started killing each other by mistake. There was a great slaughter followed by the plundering of the supplies left behind by the enemy soldiers. The story ends with the army gathering for a praise celebration, giving thanks to God for the victory he provided.

After telling that story, Alistair Begg commented that when Jehoshaphat prayed, "We do not know what to do, but our eyes are upon you," he was really saying, "Lord, we're just a bunch of pathetic losers. And if you don't help us, we're sunk." He went on to say that he had discovered that this was the true mission statement of the church he pastors: "We're just a bunch of pathetic losers; and if God doesn't help us, we're sunk." That's a good name for a church: "The Church of the Pathetic Losers." You would never run out of prospects.

Blunder forward. I think he's absolutely right. Apart from God's grace, that's all we are—just a bunch of pathetic losers. Without God we don't have a chance, we don't have a thing to offer, and we don't even know what to do next. Sometimes I think the hardest job God has is getting his children to admit how desperately they need him. So let me say clearly to everyone who reads these words: I am a pathetic loser. *Apart from the grace of God, I own up to the truth that is in me, that is in my flesh—there is nothing good at all.* Whatever talent I possess and whatever good I have accomplished, the power to do it has come from the Lord, and he alone gets the credit.

At the same pastors conference, Dr. Joseph Stowell, then president of Moody Bible Institute, commented that many days he is just sick of himself. I understand that and say "amen" to it. When I mentioned that to my own congregation, a man told me he had stayed up all night wrestling with the Lord because he too was sick of himself. A woman added, "Sometimes I get on my own nerves." And a man struggling with a cocaine addiction came to me asking for prayer that he might have the courage to share his struggles with his Sunday school class. Later I received e-mails from people who were touched by the same truth. *All of us (if we are honest) are sick of ourselves sooner or later.*

I heard about a pastor who came up with a phrase that he printed at the top of their church bulletins even though some of the leaders didn't feel comfortable with it: "Blunder Forward." Having been a pastor for over a quarter of a century, I can testify how true that is. Even on our best days, we struggle as God's people simply to "blunder forward." And some days we can't even do that. Many of us have heard the old Shaker hymn that goes like this:

> *'Tis a gift to be simple,*
> *'Tis a gift to be free,*
> *'Tis a gift to come down,*
> *Where we ought to be.*

Are we really "pathetic losers"? Yes, and we don't know the half of it. Every day we should pray, "Lord, save me from myself." By sending Elijah to the ravine, God was helping him "come down where he ought to be." The Lord does the same thing for all of us sooner or later so that we can learn that God doesn't need us but we desperately need him.

God's blessings come after we obey, not before. The NIV translates verse 5 this way: "So he did what the LORD had told him. He went to the Kerith Ravine, east of the Jordan, and stayed there" (1 Kings 17:5). What's the most important word in that verse? I'd like to nominate the last word, "there." God's command was tied to a place and to a specific act of obedience. In order to obey God,

Elijah had to do some "ravine time." Why? Because *there* is where the brook is. That's where the water is. That's where the ravens are. God is saying, "If you want my blessings, you're going to have to go *there* and stay *there*." Why? Because God's blessings come after our obedience and not before. You're going to have to go there and stay there because that's where God wants you to be.

I put it all together this way:

First there is God's command.

Then there is Elijah's obedience.

Then there is the miracle of the daily feeding by the ravens.

Command, obedience, miracle. We all like the miracle part. We all like the blessing part. We all like answered prayers. We all like the victory. But you will never get to the miracle side unless you go through the command and the obedience first. That's the point. *God's blessings came after Elijah obeyed, not before.* Years ago I ran across this statement by J. Hudson Taylor, pioneer missionary to China. "In every great work attempted for God, there are always three stages: impossible, difficult, done." The hardest step is always the first one, the impossible part. Eventually the impossible becomes difficult, and then the difficult becomes done.

God's guidance comes through suddenly changing circumstances. Verse 7 tells us that sometime later the brook dried up. Why did that happen? It was an answer to Elijah's own prayer. He had prayed that it would not rain, and the answer to that prayer brought the drought that would eventually lead the nation to repentance. Sometimes we suffer because our prayers have been answered. Your hard times don't necessarily mean you are doing something wrong. They may mean you are doing exactly what God wants you to do. Elijah obeyed God, stayed by the brook; and in answer to his own prayers, the brook eventually dried up.

What do you do when the brook dries up? *You pray and you stay and you wait.* F. B. Meyer points out that we all have to stay by a drying brook sooner or later. It may be the drying brook of popularity, or the drying brook of failing health or a sick loved one or a failing career, or the drying brook of a friendship that is slowly fading away. In some ways it is harder to sit by a drying brook than to face the prophets of Baal on Mount Carmel. Why does God allow the brook to dry up? Meyer offers this explanation: "He wants to teach us not to trust in his gifts, but in himself. He wants to drain us of self, as he drained the apostles by ten days of waiting before Pentecost. He wants to loosen our roots before he removes us to some other sphere of service and education."[4]

As we close this story, we see Elijah staying in the ravine even though the water had stopped flowing. He was there by God's command, and he will stay there until God leads him onward. The greatest scenes of Elijah's life are yet to unfold, but God knows exactly what he's doing. There is a universal truth for us if we will receive it. We must all spend some time in the ravine by the drying brook to prepare us for greater work God has for us later.

Chapter 3

ELIJAH AND THE RAVENS

"We never test the resources of God until we attempt the impossible."

R. G. LEE

Until recently, everything I knew about ravens, I learned from Edgar Allen Poe.

I don't know when I first read his poem "The Raven," but it might have been in Mrs. Graves's ninth-grade English class. All I remember about it is the spooky refrain, "Quoth the raven, 'Nevermore.'" And until I read about Elijah and ravens, I hadn't given those strange black birds another thought in almost forty years. I didn't intend to spend a whole chapter on the ravens, but for some reason I couldn't get those birds out of my mind. I thought about it and decided there must be something important here that we need to know.

So let's take a trip into the avian world and think about the ravens that fed Elijah. We begin with a few simple facts. Ravens are large black birds closely related to crows, the main difference being that ravens are bigger, with a wingspan that reaches fifty inches. They can be found from the Arctic to the deserts of North Africa to the islands of the Pacific. During flight they perform complicated aerial acrobatics. Biologists consider them to be extremely intelligent birds. But that is not their most notable characteristic. *Ravens are scavengers.* They eat berries, fruit, insects, bread, and carrion (the flesh of dead animals). They sometimes kill small birds and mammals such as rabbits and rats. They are capable of a wide range of noises, including the ability to mimic human speech. Given their black coloration, their enormous wingspan, and the fact that they are scavengers, it is no surprise that ravens have gained a mythic reputation. They have even given us a word that describes a person so hungry that he will eat anything. Such a person is said to be ravenous.[1]

Ravens appear in the Bible in only a few places. Genesis 8:6–7 says that when the floodwaters began to recede, Noah sent out a raven in search of dry land. Although the earth was still covered with water, the male raven (one-half of the entire raven population at the time) had no trouble staying alive by scavenging off all the material floating on the surface of the water. If you are raven haired, your hair is dark black. In Song of Solomon 5:11, the woman describes her beloved as having hair as "black as a raven." The scavenging side of the raven appears in Proverbs 30:17 where a rebellious child will be thrown in a valley and the ravens will pick out his eyes. Instead of an honorable burial, the rebellious child becomes food for the ravens. Isaiah prophesied that after God judged Edom, it would be so deserted that only the owl and the raven would live there (Isa. 34:11). Despite their negative image, God cares for the ravens, and he feeds them (Ps. 147:9). When Jesus wanted to impress this truth upon his disciples, he told them to "consider the ravens: They do not sow or reap, they have no storeroom or barn; yet God feeds them" (Luke 12:24 NIV).[2]

There is one more fact we need to consider. When God gave the law to Moses, he declared that ravens were unclean birds: "These are the birds you are to detest and not eat because they are detestable: the eagle, the vulture, the black vulture, the red kite, any kind of black kite, any kind of raven, the horned owl, the screech owl, the gull, any kind of hawk, the little owl, the cormorant, the great owl, the white owl, the desert owl, the osprey, the stork, any kind of heron, the hoopoe and the bat" (Lev. 11:13–19 NIV).

God doesn't say why the Jews were to consider these birds unclean ("detestable") and thus not to be eaten under any circumstances. Ravens may have been included because they eat dead flesh. But this much is certain. *Once God declared the ravens unclean, no Jew would have anything to do with them*. They were not to be eaten under any circumstances. And given their scavenging nature, that prohibition was actually a blessing to the Jews.

And that brings us back to the story of Elijah. When the Lord told him to go and hide himself by the brook Cherith on the east side of the Jordan, he also promised to send ravens to feed him. I have no doubt that the prophet was not exactly thrilled with that promise. It's hard enough to have to hide yourself in a desolate region. Far worse was the news that he would be fed twice a day by unclean birds. The whole thing was unusual because ravens normally care only for their own. Under no circumstances would they bring food to a man, much less do it twice a day.

What should we learn from the story of Elijah and the ravens?

1. God commanded and the ravens came. In 1 Kings 17:4 the Lord declares, "I have commanded the ravens to feed you there." I can imagine Elijah sitting alone by the brook when suddenly a flock of birds approaches him. They are ravens, unclean scavenger birds. It must have been a fearsome sight to see these enormous black birds swooping in with bread and meat in their beaks. But they did not come by chance, nor did they fly from a nearby cave. God sent them, God commanded them, God directed them, and thus they came to the prophet's aid.

Let me pause to ask a question. How much food does it take to sustain your family each week? I confess that I don't know the answer to that question, but my wife does. When all three of our boys lived at home, we went through an enormous amount of food every week. Some weeks we would go through five to ten gallons of milk. No matter how much we bought when we went to the grocery store, we would have to go again a few days later. That's how it is with growing boys. You have to keep feeding them because they're growing and they are always hungry. Many nights we would hear some noise in the kitchen late at night. It was Josh or Mark or Nick foraging for food. It would take some detailed calculations to figure out how much we've spent on food over the years, but God knows the exact amount because he keeps track of what we need. He knows your name, and he knows your address, and he knows what you need today, and he knows what you will need tomorrow. It's all written on his heart because he watches over you even when you think he has forgotten you. God knows what you need, and he knows when you need it, and he will make sure you have it in time. As he sent the ravens to Elijah, he can command all heaven to come to your aid.

2. *God did not allow Elijah to hoard up a surplus.* He sent the ravens to Elijah twice a day, in the morning and again in the evening. The ravens didn't bring enough on Monday to last the whole week. They brought enough in the morning to last the day and enough at night to keep him nourished during the night. Just enough and nothing more. This is what Jesus meant when he taught us to pray, "Give us this day our daily bread" (Matt. 6:11). God is teaching us in the Old Testament the same thing he is trying to teach us in the New Testament. *He is willing to supply our needs but only on a day-to-day basis.* We don't like to live like that. Most of us have freezers at home filled with food. Maybe we have a side of beef and some vegetables. We have plenty of food. There is nothing wrong with that, by the way, but a freezer filled with food makes it difficult to pray this prayer sincerely. We mutter our prayers instead of saying them from the heart because we already know we aren't going to go hungry. We don't want to live day to day. We'd rather have pension plans and stocks and bonds and options. We would rather have life insurance policies that guarantee a secure future. If we had our way, the Lord's Prayer would read, "Give us this week our weekly bread," or, "Give us this month our monthly bread." Or better yet, "Lord, give us this year our yearly bread. Just give it to us all at once and we'll be all right. Then we'll trust you." But that is not how Jesus taught us to pray, and such a prayer would not be good for us anyway. We do better when we are forced to depend on God every day.

Life *is* uncertain. Most of us don't have enough savings to get through more than another month or so. You can be doing fine, and then one day the doctor says, "I'm sorry the tests are positive.

You've got cancer." Your life gets rearranged in a split second. Just when you think you've got it all together, an illness, the loss of a job, the collapse of an empire that you put together can happen so fast. God lets those things happen to move us from self-sufficiency to God sufficiency. From self-reliance to God reliance. From trusting in our own ability to trusting in him alone.

One Day at a Time

I talked with a single mother who ran her own business. When I asked how things were going, she smiled and said, "We're barely making it. June was tough. But I've got two jobs for July. We're going to be OK for July. That's the way it is. Just when we're about to run out, God brings us a little more work." That's not easy, but she has discovered something that those of us who have plenty of money never discover. She's learning in the laboratory of life that God *will* meet her needs.

Am I saying that we shouldn't plan ahead? No, I'm not saying that. You should plan ahead. That's biblical. You should plan ahead, but you shouldn't worry ahead. There's a big difference. Here is how Charles Spurgeon brought the truth home:

> Elijah had enough, but it did not always come to him in the nicest way; for I do not imagine that the ravens knew how to get bread and meat always cut into nicest shape. Perhaps they snatched a rough bit of meat here, and perhaps a crust of bread there, and it came in all sorts of ugly pieces, but still, there it was, and it was enough. "Beggars are not to be choosers," we say, and certainly pensioners on God's bounty ought not pick holes and find fault with the Lord's providing. Whatever

God gives thee be grateful for, for if too proud to take from the raven's mouth, it will be well for thee to go without, until hunger consume thy pride. God promises his people enough, but not more than enough, and even that enough may not come to us in the way we should choose.[3]

3. *God didn't ask Elijah's permission before he sent the ravens.* I'm sure he didn't ask because I think Elijah would have said, "Lord, I've got a better idea." Ravens are scavengers whose number one meal is decaying flesh. They are flying garbage disposals. No respectable Jew would eat a raven, and neither would we. How would you respond if someone said, "Why don't you come over this Saturday, and we'll have some fried raven and mashed potatoes?" I think you'd find a reason to be somewhere else. Perhaps Elijah wondered where the ravens got the food they brought him. Did they pick apart some decaying carcass and bring the leftovers to the prophet of God?

No, it wasn't like that at all. The same God who commanded the ravens made sure that the food they brought Elijah was good for him. *In this we see both the creativity and the sovereignty of God.* He can take an unclean bird and feed his prophet, and he can do it for days or months or even for years. James 5:17 says that because of Elijah's prayers, it did not rain in Israel for three and a half years. If that's how long he was at Cherith, it means that the ravens served him more than two thousand meals.

We would have been less surprised if God had used a sparrow or a robin to bring the food. But that is not how God works. *He routinely chooses the despised things of the world in order to confound the mighty, and he uses the foolish to bring the strong down to nothing.* As you look at the course of life, you may think that God is going to use some rich uncle or a wealthy friend to help you out. But experience shows how unlikely that is. He is much more likely to meet your needs through the ravens of the earth that fly to your need when you least expect them. The Lord has plenty of ravens to supply the needs of his children. If God sends you to Cherith to hide you for a season, do not despair, for he has not forgotten you. Though you be hidden to man, you are not hidden to your heavenly Father. He knows where you are, and he knows why you are there. Your grocery list is written on his heart. Do not be surprised when a flock of large black birds gathers to your hiding place. They are God's ravens, sent from heaven to bring you food.

4. *God has appointed the beginning and ending of every season of life.* First Kings 17:7 says that "some time later the brook dried up" (NIV). That makes it sound as if it happened by chance. But the Hebrew phrase translated "some time later" actually means "at the end of days." It means the brook dried at the end of the days appointed by God. The water ran as long as God decreed, and on the day he decreed, the brook began to dry up. Remember the words of Psalm 115:3, "Our God is in heaven; he does whatever pleases him" (NIV). All creation must answer to him. Every drop of water that falls comes from his hand. The same God who sent the rain also sent the drought. The same God who called Elijah to confront Ahab also sent him to hide by the brook. The same God who sent the ravens now sends him to live with the widow of Zarephath. As the narrative of Elijah's life unfolds, it appears to take many wild swings.

> From the mountains of Gilead,
> To the king's palace,
> To the brook Cherith,
> To a widow's home in Zarephath.

But what seems to be haphazard and unplanned is actually the unfolding of God's divine plan. "In his heart a man plans his course, but the LORD determines his steps" (Prov. 16:9 NIV). Most of our plans don't stand. They are like the leaves that blow away in the autumn wind. *But when God determines to do something, it will happen.* You can write it down and take it to the bank. You can make all the speeches you want and announce your long-range plans, your ten-year goals, and your personal objectives, but just remember this: When you are finished, God always gets the last word. What a relief to realize that God is God and we're not. Now you can rip that big G off your sweatshirt. You don't have to play God anymore, and you don't have to try to control everything around you. *You can sleep well when you realize that God is God and you are not.* Corrie Ten Boom was having trouble going to sleep one night because she was so worried about the affairs of her life. She tried praying, but it didn't help. Finally, the Lord said to her, "Go to sleep, Corrie. I'm going to be up all night anyway."

Philip Yancey's Definition

But it won't always be easy or come quickly. For most of us, most of the time, the exact opposite will be true. Discovering God's will takes time as the events of life unfold before us, often in ways that seem to make no sense at all. Rarely will we know the whole plan in advance. And as I've already pointed, that's actually a good thing. As I sit at my computer and ponder the course of my life over the last decade, I find it easier to recall the hard times than the good times. I remember a painful controversy in the church that led to broken friendships and misunderstanding. Several close friends died suddenly and without warning. My youngest son went through a harrowing medical crisis that threatened his life, and in various forms it continues to this day. But that's only one side of the ledger. In the last decade our three boys graduated from high school and college, all three have spent time in China, and our oldest son has gotten married to a wonderful girl. I am blessed with a wife of amazing gifts who still loves me after thirty-two years of marriage. The Lord has opened wonderful doors for ministry. My health is good. So what do I have to complain about? Not much at all. Ten years ago I had no clue what the next decade would hold. Looking back, I'm happy that I didn't know anything in advance.

My favorite definition of *faith* comes from Philip Yancey, who said, "Faith means believing in advance what will only make sense in reverse." We want to know why things happen the way they do and why things couldn't have happened some other way. It would be wrong to say that faith provides all the answers. It doesn't. Perhaps in heaven we will fully understand, or in heaven our desire to know will be transformed by our vision of the Lord. By faith we see things that are invisible to others, and by faith we believe in advance those things that right now make no sense but one day will make perfect sense because we will view them in reverse.

The world says, "Seeing is believing." God says, "Believing is seeing." We believe, therefore we see.

When You Need to Know, You'll Know

I saw this principle in action several years ago when a young couple, recently graduated from Moody Bible Institute, came to see me. They had just finished the first part of a training course with a missions organization in the Chicago area. Their advisor told them they needed to talk with their pastor before taking the next step. So they came to see me with the good news that God was calling them to the mission field.

"Where do you want to go?" I asked.

"We don't know," the husband replied.

So I looked at the wife, and she smiled in agreement.

"You mean you have no idea at all?"

"No idea at all."

Then I held up my hand and moved it as if I were twirling a globe. "You mean that in all the world, you don't have even a tiny idea where you would like to go?"

"No."

That does make it difficult when you are trying to raise funds because they couldn't answer the first question: "Where do you plan to go?" I sat there silently for a moment, pondering the situation. No one had ever said anything like that to me before. Suddenly I had a flash of inspiration. Looking right at that young couple, I said, "I've got the answer. The reason you don't know is because you don't need to know because if you needed to know, you would know; but since you don't know, you must not need to know because if you had needed to know by now, you would know by now; but since you don't know, you must not need to know because when you need to know, you'll know. If God is God, that must be true." They were dazzled and speechless, and I was pretty amazed myself because all of that just came popping out at the spur of the moment. We prayed and they left my office, still smiling.

Not long after that, I happened to meet a young lady from our church who works at Moody Bible Institute. She had a job in the music library that was scheduled to come to an end in a few months. Our paths crossed in the sanctuary lobby between services. When I asked her what she planned to do next, she said she had no idea. So on the spur of the moment I decided to try it again. "The reason you don't know is because you don't need to know because if you needed to know, you would know; but since you don't know, you must not need to know because if you had needed to know by now, you would know by now; but since you don't know, you must not need to know because when you need to know, you'll know. If God is God, that must be true." She laughed and said that sounded right. And off she went.

Several weeks later when I saw her again, she had a big smile on her face. "Pastor Ray, you won't believe what happened. I was talking with a friend about things, and my friend asked me if I had ever considered going to the mission field. I said no, and she said I should think about it. I'm a music librarian. What would I do on the mission field? But a few days later I happened to pass by a missions display and saw a representative sitting there. Normally I would just walk right by, but this time I stopped to talk. When I asked if they ever needed librarians on the mission field, the man said, 'Absolutely! We could use some librarians right now.' So I started doing some research, and on a Web site I discovered a Christian school in Kenya that needed a librarian starting exactly when I finish my job at Moody. I e-mailed them, they e-mailed back, and they checked my references. And guess what, Pastor Ray, I got the job! I'm moving to Nairobi, Kenya, in late July to get started as the librarian for a Christian school." As of this writing, she has returned to the United States after spending five happy years in Kenya. She recently wrote to say that she is once again waiting on the Lord for his direction: "When I need to know, I'll know."

A few weeks later the young couple came back to see me with similar good news. "We're going to Russia."

"No kidding. Russia, that's great. Did you know about this when you came to see me?"

"No, we had no idea."

"So where in Russia are you going?"

"We're going to the Black Sea."

"That's fantastic. What are you going to do there?"

"We're going to teach in a school and help with church planting."

When I asked them how they ended up going to the Black Sea to teach and do church planting, they told me a story that was so detailed it was positively Byzantine in its complexity. They met someone who knew someone who "happened" to know a woman whom they met almost by chance. She came over to talk to them, and one thing led to another, and now they were going to Russia. I couldn't draw it on a chart if I tried. But they were so happy about it, and I was happy for them. They are currently involved in their ministry near the Black Sea, teaching and helping plant churches.

I am amazed as I think about how God led that young woman and that young couple to Kenya and Russia, respectively. But on second thought, why be amazed? That's how God works, isn't it? When you need to know, you'll know. Not one day sooner, not one day later. And if today you don't know what to do next, it's because you truly don't need to know. Because if you needed to know, you would know. If God is God, that must be true.

That's how God works with all of us.

He sends Elijah to the brook.

Then he sends the ravens.

When the time comes, the brook dries up.

And Elijah moves on to his next assignment from the Lord.

He doesn't see any of this in advance. It's always on a "need to know" basis.

When you need to know, you'll know.

Meanwhile enjoy the brook and be grateful for the ravens.

Would you like to be like Elijah? I met a woman who told me she prays, "Lord, do the impossible in my life." That's an Elijah-like prayer because the prophet continually saw things happen that could not be explained apart from God. If we are willing to obey, God will take care of the details. He can send the ravens to feed us when the world has forgotten us.

Chapter 4

ℰMPTY BARREL
GRADUATE SCHOOL

"One who believes the Lord has called him and given him a gift to preach and teach, need not be hasty or anxious. Power makes itself felt, and it is well to begin in a small way."
WILLIAM KELLY

ℐn the last few years China has become important to our family because God has called all three of our sons to China, at least for the short-term. Our oldest son spent a year teaching English in Beijing and came back to America completely transformed. Our youngest son spent a summer teaching English in China and now hopes to take a graduate degree in Chinese studies. Our middle son is currently in China teaching English for at least two years. My wife and I have been there twice. So China is on our minds all the time. In the last two years I've read more about China than in all the previous years of my life put together.

Several months ago a friend gave me a little paperback book called *China Travail* that has been out of print for quite a few years. The book tells the story of William Englund, pioneer missionary to China in the first half of the twentieth century. He arrived in China in 1903 and stayed until the Communists came to power in 1949. Something I read early in the book made me think of Elijah's story. When William Englund and his new bride of eight weeks arrived in Shanghai, they immediately set out for the mission station in the city of Sian, 650 miles away. That would be a long day's drive for most of us. In 1903 it meant traveling for many days on a riverboat, followed by many weeks riding mules along the rutted dirt roads. Here is a brief description of that trip:

> Slung in a hammock-like contraption secured to two beasts of capacious temperament and uncertain cooperation, William Englund and Lena Englund had plenty of leisure to meditate on what might be ahead. What his own imagination lacked was supplied by other travelers in wild tales of hairbreadth escapes from robbers related over sputtering oil lamps in the inns where they took lodging each night. Such experiences were to become routine, but he was glad when the high broad walls of Sian eventually broke the monotony of the otherwise uninterrupted dusty horizons. It took William Englund and his new bride two months to travel six hundred and fifty miles. Two months was a long time for so short a journey, and it well illustrated the old Chinese proverb: Don't worry about going slowly; only fear coming to a complete stop. Truly the days had not been wasted. By prayer, study, and with considerable help from Lena,

William Englund had gone through a primer printed by the China Inland Mission and had become familiar with some of the basics of Chinese. He was ready for a study in depth of that fascinating language.[1]

Two months is indeed a long time to travel 650 miles, but don't worry about going slowly. Only fear coming to a complete stop. When last we left our hero, he was alone by the brook Cherith on the east side of the Jordan River. He had been there for a long time. Famine had come to the land in answer to his own prayers. And because the rains had stopped, the brook had dried up, which meant he could not stay there forever. But he was not yet ready to confront Ahab and the prophets of Baal. Having seen the king once, he had now gone into hiding at the Lord's command. Before he was ready to go face the prophets of Baal, there was one more stop he must make.

Four Tests for Elijah

God had some testing in store for his servant. "Then the word of the LORD came to him: 'Go at once to Zarephath of Sidon and stay there. I have commanded a widow in that place to supply you with food'" (1 Kings 17:8–9 NIV). Before Elijah would be ready for the big challenge on Mount Carmel, there were four tests he must pass.

1. The Test of a New Place—Zarephath was a small village in Sidon, in the region of modern-day Lebanon. It was north of the land of Israel. The geography matters because there is someone else in this story who came from Sidon. Her name was Jezebel, Ahab's pagan wife. Sidon was a center of Baal worship. And now God was taking his servant from the brook Cherith and sending him to Zarephath in Sidon. To get there he had to travel into Gentile territory, into the region of Baal worship; and when he got there, he was somehow to meet a widow who would tell him what to do next. Verse 10 tells us Elijah's response: "So Elijah got up and went to Zarephath. When he arrived at the city gate, there was a widow woman gathering wood" (HCSB). Note a couple of things. The word *Zarephath* comes from the Hebrew word for smelting place, meaning it once housed a furnace where they produced iron by heating the ore until the iron separated from the dross. The iron would then be used for the construction of weapons and chariots. Elijah was being sent from the brook into the furnace, so to speak. Consider how difficult this must have been.

He was to go and meet a woman. In that culture that was not easy to do.

He was to go and meet a Gentile woman. For a Jewish man that was doubly difficult.

He was to go and meet a Gentile woman who was a widow. This meant that when he found her, she was going to be very poor.

And notice one other thing. God told Elijah to go to Zarephath and "stay there." First he was to stay by the brook. Then he was to stay in a widow's house in Zarephath. That's not an easy command for a man of action like Elijah. Elijah had been by himself for a long time, hiding by the brook. The brook had dried up, and God had sent him into Baal's backyard. His orders were simple: Stay there.

Do you ever feel like God got your file messed up with somebody else's file? Recently I researched the Internet to see how many people named Ray Pritchard I could find. I typed the word *ray* into a search engine and discovered there are 437 million pages on the Internet containing that word. But *ray* might refer to a shaft of light, not just to a person. So I tried *Pritchard* and discovered there are almost 13 million Web pages containing my family name. Then I tried *Ray* and *Pritchard* together and learned there are 1.3 million pages containing both of those words. When I put *Ray Pritchard* in quotes, I learned there are 85,000 pages containing my name. Most of those refer to some other "Ray Pritchard." It's easy to imagine someone looking for one Ray Pritchard but calling another one by mistake. Sometimes it's easy to think that the filing system on the heavenly computer went haywire somehow. You can imagine Elijah thinking something like this: *Lord, I have been here long enough, and now you are sending me into Gentile territory to find a widow who is dirt poor, and you want me to stay there. I am called to preach the Word, and I am called to bring the nation back to you. Lord, what are you doing?* It can be humbling, and it can be frustrating when God says, "Stay where you are."

"Lord, I want to go someplace else."

"Stay there."

"Lord, I don't like this job."

"Stay there."

"Lord, I don't really like my neighbors."

"Stay there."

"Lord, I'm not too happy in my marriage."

"Stay there."

"Lord, I'm tired of my church."

"Stay there."

It can be frustrating when you're in a job, in a relationship, in a situation where you are ready to go and God says stay there.

The first test was the test of a new place. Not just are you willing to go there, Elijah, but are you willing to go and stay there?

2. The Test of First Impressions—"'Go at once to Zarephath of Sidon and stay there. I have commanded a widow in that place to supply you with food.' So he went to Zarephath. When he came to the town gate, a widow was there gathering sticks" (vv. 9–10 NIV). That's about as hopeless a situation as you could find. A widow dressed in a widow's garb gathering sticks. Elijah doesn't offer to help her. Instead he asks her to help him. "He called to her and asked, 'Would you bring me a little water in a jar so I may have a drink?' As she was going to get it, he called, 'And bring me, please, a piece of bread'" (vv. 10–11 NIV). This may seem heartless, but it is the only way the prophet can know for sure if she is the widow God intended him to meet. Her response reveals that she is the right one: "'As surely as the LORD your God lives,' she replied, 'I don't have any bread—only a handful of flour in a jar and a little oil in a jug. I am gathering a few sticks to take home and make a meal for myself and my son, that we may eat it—and die'" (v. 12 NIV). Things aren't looking hopeful for the prophet of God. When he gets to Zarephath, he meets a widow who is gathering sticks to cook one final meal after which she and her son will starve to death. This happens more often than you would think. When Abraham arrived in the land of Canaan, what is the first thing that happened? According to Genesis 12, there was a famine in the land. After taking that enormous step of faith and leaving Ur of the Chaldees, after traversing the desert with his caravan, and after finally arriving in the promised land, suddenly there was a famine in the land. So he and his wife Sarah moved to Egypt. That's the way it goes sometimes.

- So you say to yourself, *My job stinks and my boss is a jerk. I'm going to get a new job.* And lo and behold, you get a new job, and your new boss is twice the jerk your old boss was. There's a famine in the promised land.
- You say to yourself, *I'm sick of this old house. I'm going to buy a new house.* And the first time it rains, you realize your foundation is cracked because your basement is flooded. There's a famine in the promised land.
- You leave your old church for a new church, and the people aren't very friendly. There's a famine in the promised land.

It's amazing how often there's a famine in the promised land. You think, *If I change my circumstances, things are going to get better.* Don't count on it. Change isn't bad. Sometimes we need to make a change. But change doesn't always improve your outward circumstances.

Here is the test we all have to face. *Am I willing to obey God even when it doesn't make a whole lot of sense?* When you are called by God to speak to the nation, it doesn't make sense to go spend a long time hiding by the brook, and it makes even less sense to go to Zarephath and meet some widow who is down to her last meal. That's not what you would call upward career mobility. But it's in the Bible. There's a whole lot of life that doesn't make sense. Sooner or later there's a famine in the promised land. It's not a bad thing; it's a test from God because if God made it easy, we'd take him for granted. If God made it easy, we wouldn't pray so much. If God made it easy, we'd think better of ourselves than we should. When there's a famine in the promised land, you get on your knees and you start praying.

It's a wonderful thing when your children do well. But when your children are struggling, it doesn't make any difference how rich you are. All the money in the world means nothing when your kids are struggling. And when they're doing good, money doesn't mean anything anyway. There are times when there's a famine in the promised land with your kids, and that too is allowed by God to keep us on our knees daily, crying out to the Lord. It's a test. It's not a judgment. It's a test to see whether we will still believe. It's not hard to praise God when you've got money in the bank, the boss just gave you a raise, your marriage is happy, your kids are doing fine, and all is right in the world. But if all you've got is a God of the good times, you do not have the God of the Bible, and you don't have faith that will help you in the hard times. What are you going to do when the boss says, "You're fired," when you run out of money, when the doctor says, "I'm sorry, it's cancer, and there's nothing we can do"? What are you going to do when your wife or husband says, "I'm finished with this marriage"? What are you going to do when your kids are struggling? In those moments, you really find out what you're all about. All of us are going to spend some time in the furnace.

A friend who is struggling with cancer writes to say that her combined chemotherapy and radiation treatments have turned into a difficult ordeal. This is her second time around so her body is a bit weaker, and the prognosis remains unclear. At the moment she has radiation burns plus she is anemic so she has very little energy. After writing a paragraph about her symptoms, she ends with a one-word commentary: "Sigh."

Where do you find hope in moments like this? My friends quoted a few verses from the book of Habakkuk, a little gem hidden away in the section of the Old Testament we call the Minor

Prophets. The word *minor* refers to the length of the book (only three chapters), not to the importance of the message. After Habakkuk surveys the moral and spiritual desolation of his day, and the confusion about what God is trying to say to his people, he ends his message with these ringing words:

> Though the fig tree does not bud
> and there are no grapes on the vines,
> though the olive crop fails
> and the fields produce no food,
> though there are no sheep in the pen
> and no cattle in the stalls,
> yet I will rejoice in the LORD,
> I will be joyful in God my Savior.
> The Sovereign LORD is my strength;
> he makes my feet like the feet of a deer,
> he enables me to go on the heights
> (Hab. 3:17–19 NIV).

Sometimes the fig tree does not bud.
Sometimes there are no grapes on the vine.
Sometimes the olive crop fails.
Sometimes the fields produce no food.
Sometimes there are no sheep in the pen.
Sometimes there are no cattle in the stalls.

Sometimes life deals you a bad set of cards. What do you do then? You can get angry with God, or you can give up on God altogether. Or you can conclude that God doesn't know what he's doing. Or that the universe has spun out of God's control. Or you do what Habakkuk did, and what my friend is doing: You can choose to believe in God anyway. Often we mistake faith and our feelings. Faith isn't about my feelings, much less about my circumstances. Faith is a conscious choice I make, a moment-by-moment decision to believe that God is fully involved in my situation regardless of my current circumstances. Faith chooses to believe when it would be easier to stop believing. Habakkuk said, "I *will* rejoice," and, "I *will* be joyful." My friend says the same thing. Therefore, the prophet found new strength in the midst of desolation, confusion, loss, discouragement, and the frustration of adverse circumstances.

Chemotherapy is no fun, and radiation isn't a walk in the park. My friend knows that truth firsthand. She would tell you that she is in a fight for her life. But she has chosen to believe and chosen to rejoice. Like Mary of old, she has "chosen the better part" and has received the blessing reserved for those who choose to keep believing when times are tough.

Elijah had to go to Zarephath, the smelting place. He had to spend some time in a desperate situation. Why? It was good for him. He needed it. He needed to stay with a widow because she taught him compassion. There was no other way for him to learn it.

3. *The Test of a Hopeless Situation*—This poor widow is gathering sticks to prepare a final meal before she and her son die together. If ever there was an impossible situation, here it is. Elijah said to her, "Don't be afraid." I'm sure she was glad to hear that. Then he gave her some strange instructions. "Go home and do as you have said. But first make a small cake of bread for me from what you have and bring it to me, and then make something for yourself and your son. For this is what the LORD, the God of Israel, says: 'The jar of flour will not be used up and the jug of oil will not run dry until the day the LORD gives rain on the land'" (1 Kings 17:13–14 NIV). From a human point of view, this makes no sense whatsoever. By every standard of reasonable calculation,

this poor widow and her son will soon starve to death. All the evidence pointed in that direction. Elijah had only two things to go on at this point. *First, he had the memory of what God had done in the past. Second, he had God's Word in the present.* He remembered how God had taken care of him by the brook, and he knew that God had called him, and so he knew that somehow God would take care of him, and God would take care of that widow and her son. It must have been hard for him to say those words. It must have been hard for her to hear those words. But somehow she had faith to believe what Elijah said.

4. *The Test of Obedient Faith*—The Bible says in verse 15 that "she went away and did as Elijah told her" (NIV). Literally the Hebrew says, "She went and did." Here is the end of the story: "So there was food every day for Elijah and for the woman and her family. For the jar of flour was not used up and the jug of oil did not run dry, in keeping with the word of the LORD spoken by Elijah" (vv. 15–16 NIV). This was a pure miracle from God. When the barrel is full of oil, you don't need faith because you've got all the oil you need. Faith comes in when you are almost out and you don't know how you're going to go to fill it up again. That's when you find out how much faith you have.

Personally I much prefer when the barrel is full of oil. You don't have to worry so much. You don't have to think about where the next meal is coming from. It's good when the barrel is full of oil. I like opening the refrigerator and finding it full of food, especially when I'm hungry in the middle of the night. I like it when I open the freezer and find four kinds of ice cream ready for me to sample. It's not so good when the barrel of oil is nearly empty. But in the kingdom of God, the values of life are completely reversed, which is why this story speaks to modern

Christians, especially to Western Christians who live in such prosperity compared to the rest of the world. *For the people of God, abundance is generally much more dangerous than lack.* That's why Jesus said it is hard for a rich man to enter the kingdom of heaven (Matt. 19:23)—not because money is bad, but when you have money, you depend upon it. And that is why the poor often respond quickly to the gospel, and those who have a lot often don't feel their need for God because their barrel is full. Although I prefer to live with a full barrel, God often lets the barrel run out because it's better for me to live in want than in abundance.

"God Must Love You Very Much"

Elijah's journey demonstrates that God often multiplies his tests. We finish one test and bam! Here comes another one. God does it to keep us humble. He does it to purify us. He does it because we need it even though we don't like it very much. First he sends us to Dry Brook University; and as soon as we are finished there, he enrolls us in Empty Barrel Graduate School. Why? *God sends the tests to make us stronger.* Once we are stronger, we are ready to take the next step. Nothing in Elijah's life happens by chance. Every step has been ordered by the Lord to prepare him for greater work to come. From the mountains to the palace to the brook and now to the widow's home in Zarephath. God was preparing his man every step along the way.

God does the same thing for you and me. Some of us are by the brook, and the water is running out. You may be in Zarephath, and the oil and the flour are about gone. You may feel that God is punishing you or that God has forgotten you. Instead, the Lord says, "My child, I love you, and I have plans to give you a hope and a future. When I am finished, you will be ready for the next step." Not long ago I ran across a statement that summed up this truth for me:

We teach what we know; we reproduce what we are.

Through the long months by the brook and in Zarephath, God was building character into Elijah's life that could be reproduced in other people. Let's pause to consider what Elijah learned at Cherith and Zarephath:

At Cherith Elijah learned, "God can take care of me."

At Zarephath he learned, "God can use me to take care of others."

Elijah needed the brook, and he needed the widow's house because they taught him lessons he couldn't learn any other way. That leads me to make a simple application.

When God says go, don't analyze it. Just go.

When God says stay, don't analyze it. Just stay.

A woman with many problems felt as if her life was falling to pieces, and so a friend said, "There's a convent nearby. Why don't you go there for a prayer retreat?" On the first day, she got on the elevator to go to her room on the fourth floor. Just before the doors closed, a nun walked into the elevator with her. The nun looked at the woman and said, "My dear, why have you come to this place?" And almost without thinking, the woman blurted out, "My mother has just died. I think my father is an alcoholic. My marriage is in trouble, and I'm afraid I am losing my mind." She said all of that as the elevator was going from the first floor to the third floor. The door opened on the third floor, and the nun started to get out, but before she did, she turned to the woman and said, "God must love you very much." Then she walked on out of the elevator, and the doors closed.[2]

I think that nun was on to something important. What is God saying through the trials and struggles of life? One thing he is saying is, "I love you more than you know. I'm going to send you to the brook, and I'll take care of you there. I'm going to send you into the furnace, and I'll go into the furnace with you there. I'll be with you in the hard times, and when those hard times are done, I will bring you out, and you'll be prepared for the next step in our journey together."

I am not saying that God loves you in spite of your hard times. I am saying that your hard times prove that God really does love you.

He loves you more than you know.

He loves you unreasonably.

He loves you despite all your failures.

He loves you so much that he won't let you stay the way you are.

Hard times force us to get down to the bottom line of life, to that desperation point where we discover what we truly believe. No one likes to be there, and no one wants to stay there, but God knows what he is doing even when we think he has forgotten about us. We've all got to do some "ravine time" and some "furnace time." It's part of his preparation to make you what he wants you to be so that like Elijah, when the moment comes, you'll be ready to take the next step with him.

Chapter 5

ℛESURRECTION HOSPITAL

*"I know God will not give me anything I can't handle.
I just wish that he didn't trust me so much."*
MOTHER TERESA

A young man died in a car accident, leaving his friends heartbroken and confused. I was asked to write to one of those friends to offer whatever encouragement I could. I was glad to do it, and as I did so, I thought about how often I have done that. Years ago I struggled with what to say in a situation of sudden death. Looking back, I think I felt the burden of trying to explain what happened so that the faith of those left behind would not be shattered. But that burden is far too heavy for me. I don't know why things happen the way they do. I suppose the difference now is that I don't feel embarrassed saying that I don't know. And I've found it doesn't bother people when I tell the truth about my inability to explain the great mysteries of life and death.

Last year a dear friend died in circumstances that were hard to accept. I've thought of his death a lot since then, and I still don't understand it.

When we moved to Mississippi, it was deer-hunting season. A man in his forties came by to say that he would be hunting on my brother's property. He was pleasant, friendly, handsome; and he exuded a casual self-confidence that made you feel at ease in his presence. Later he shot a deer on our property and gave us some of the meat. Once or twice more he came around, and we chatted briefly. A few weeks ago his teenage son and a friend were driving late at night on one of the many country roads near Tupelo. The driver lost control of the car. They were going over one hundred miles per hour when the car hit a tree, killing both young men instantly.

Yesterday I heard about a friend I hadn't seen in many years who died unexpectedly a day or so after surgery.

Few things in life are more difficult than the sudden death of a friend. And when it happens in some sort of accident, the mind wrestles with so many unanswerable questions, chief among them *why*. Why did things happen the way they did and when they did? And why should a young man just starting out have his life so quickly cut short?

I have learned that where you start makes all the difference in thinking about sickness, suffering, and death. If you start with the accident or with the sickness or with death itself, you will never come to the right answer. I know many people whose faith has been badly shaken and even destroyed by the tragedies of life. I know that feeling myself. If you start at the tragedy and try to reason your way back to God, you won't make it. You'll fall off the ladder somewhere. None of us is smart enough to reason from a tragedy back to God. The only hope is to start at the other end, with what we know to be true about God. If you start with God, if you remember who he is and why he sent his Son to the earth, and his wisdom, power, goodness, and love, if you start there, you can slowly make your way back to the tragedy itself. I have walked that road myself many times. This is not some sort of magic trick that will make the pain go away (it won't) or answer all your questions (it won't do that either), but starting with God provides the only possible framework for answering the questions we all have.

We need a God so big, so great, so powerful, so wise, so vast, so eternal that he can encompass the sudden death of one of his children. Some people talk as if the tragedies of life are accidents in the universe. As if God turned his head away and something bad happened while God wasn't looking. As if God tried to stop it but couldn't. A God like that is no God at all. I cannot worship an impotent, puny, man-made God who abdicates the throne of the universe and leaves us alone in our despair. That is not the God of the Bible.

Here are two Scriptures to meditate on. The first comes from Isaiah 53:10 in the New American Standard Bible: "But the LORD was pleased to crush Him, putting Him to grief." Isaiah is speaking of the Father's decision to put his Son to death on the cross for the sins of the world. Think about what that says. Not just that the Father sent his Son to die or that he allowed his Son to die. It is much stronger than that. In ways that we cannot fathom, it pleased the Lord to allow his Son to suffer and die. How can any father be pleased to crush his own son? I cannot imagine it. Parents do all they can to protect their children. But our Father was pleased, for the sake of our salvation, to crush his own Son. That tells us that God's ways and our ways are not the same, and we cannot judge him by human standards. The second verse is Psalm 115:3, "Our God is in heaven; he does whatever pleases him" (NIV). God does what he wants, and no one can stop him. Here we come up against the bedrock of God himself. He is great and powerful beyond our imagining. All that he does is right, even those things we do not understand.

And that brings us to the story of the death of the widow's son in 1 Kings 17:17–24. Of all the episodes in the life of Elijah, this is probably the most troublesome. In our text Elijah lays himself out over the body of a dead child, and the boy comes back to life. And it's not exactly like the story of the resurrection of our Lord on Easter Sunday morning, which is surrounded by angels and a sense of glorious triumph. It doesn't even carry with it the same feel of Jesus crying out, "Lazarus, come forth" (John 11:43 KJV). Because this story is so unusual, some people have discounted it as being a myth. They see it as a kind of folk story, almost like a fairy tale. Some liberal scholars, who do not take the miracle stories of the Bible literally, suggest that either the boy wasn't really dead or that it never really happened at all. Before we examine this passage, I want you to know that I firmly believe exactly what the Bible says. I think the widow's son died, Elijah stretched himself over the boy's body and prayed, God heard his prayer, and the boy's life returned to him. But I also acknowledge the emotional difficulties because it raises questions we don't often talk about. If God can do this some of the time, why doesn't he do this all the time? That is a great question, but I don't know how you can deal with the story without coming to grips with some of the great mysteries of God in his mercy and sovereignty, what God does and what God doesn't do. We'll look at that in just a moment.

A Mother's Sorrow

The story begins this way:

"Some time later the son of the woman who owned the house became ill. He grew worse and worse, and finally he stopped breathing. She said to Elijah, 'What do you have against me, man of God? Did you come to remind me of my sin and kill my son?'" (1 Kings 17:17–18 NIV).

Note carefully the first phrase, "Some time later." The Hebrew literally says, "After these things it happened." That's a powerful statement about God's sovereignty. Whatever else you want to say about this unforgettable episode, don't call it an accident. The child didn't get sick by chance, and he didn't die by chance. His sickness and his death were both part of the sovereign plan of God.

There are so many mysteries about why God does what he does. I'm reminded of the words of Tony Evans, who said, "Everything in the universe is either caused by God or allowed by God, and there is no third category." That's a hugely important statement. So many times we look at heartbreaking tragedy, and we want to invent a third category called, "Bad things that just happened for no reason." But there is no such category. When the text says that it came about that the child grew ill, it's the writer's way of saying that what happened to this young boy was not an accident. It was not chance. It was not fate. God was present in the home when that boy died.

The timing of all this deserves our attention. The boy got sick after many weeks and months of miraculous provision by God. After many months of the flour and the oil never running out, suddenly the boy got sick and died. Why does it happen that way? We walk with the Lord and we do the best we can, and one day the phone call comes that changes life forever. Or we get a report from the doctor with bad news. Or our children get into terrible trouble. Or our marriage falls apart. Why do these things happen?

It is very easy for us to become complacent in the midst of the blessings of God. We secretly begin to think: *Everything's OK now; I've got life all wired up. My marriage is good, and my kids are good, and my job is good, and life is good, and I love my church. Everything in my life is exactly where I want it to be.* If that happens to be your situation at this moment, don't feel bad about that. If your life is like that, you ought to enjoy it, and you ought to be profoundly grateful to God. But know these two things for certain:

1. You don't deserve these blessings.

2. They won't last forever.

They never do. Soon enough the clouds will move in, and the rain begins to fall. You shouldn't live in fear, but you ought to be wise enough to know that after sunrise comes sundown, and after high noon comes the darkness of midnight. So it is for all of us sooner or later.

After the time of God's blessing, disaster strikes. We don't know why the child got sick. It almost seems like a contradiction. There was the testing, then the blessing, and then the sorrow. It seems like it ought to be reversed, turned around somehow, like it ought to be sorrow and then testing and then blessing. But that's not how God works. It's more often this way:

Testing

Blessing

Sorrow

It is so easy to be lulled into false thinking. *Ah, we made it through the hard times. It's going to be smooth sailing from here on out.* But that usually is not God's design for us.

A Period Before the End of the Sentence

Of all the sorrows of life, I know of no sorrow greater than the death of a child. Nothing seems more unnatural. Parents are not supposed to bury their children. It is the privilege and the honor of children to bury their parents. It is not supposed to be the other way around. *The death of a child is like a period before the end of the sentence.* Several years ago I was called to the hospital because an eleven-day-old baby had died during the night. As I drove to the hospital, it occurred to me that when I was new in the ministry, I used to dread these moments. It's only in later years that I've come to understand that this is really what the ministry is all about. Preaching and teaching may be the most visible part of the ministry, but it's not the whole thing. The real work is going to the hospital to comfort brokenhearted parents. Somewhere along the way the Lord just took my fear away. In my early years I was always afraid I'd say the wrong thing. *After a while I learned the less you say the better.* When I got to the hospital, they ushered me into a small room where the parents were holding their little baby in their arms, and they had been weeping. When I walked into the room, they both stood up. The father said, "Pastor Ray, I'm so glad to see you." Later he told me, "When you walked into the room, it was like Jesus walked into the room." That's one of the great honors of being a pastor, to bring the Lord into a situation like that.

We sat down, and I looked at the tiny body of that baby. We talked for a minute, and then the mother started weeping. At one point tears ran off her face and fell onto the forehead of her little child. She was rocking back and forth as she said to me, "God has a reason, doesn't he?" I took a deep breath and said, "God does have a reason, but I don't know what it is." In the early days of my ministry I would have given a long explanation that would have done no good. I since have learned if you don't know, you might as well just say you don't know.

I don't know why that child died any more than I know why the widow's son died. The mother's dreams were dashed. She didn't see this coming at all. If you go back and read the text, she thought she and her son would die together because of the famine in the land. In her anguish and in her sorrow, she blamed Elijah. "What do you have against me, man of God? Did you come to remind me of my sin and kill my son?" (1 Kings 17:18 NIV). There are at least three problems with her thinking. *First, she seems to have thought that having a prophet in the house made her immune from suffering.* Who could blame her, especially after all the miraculous provision of the flour and the oil? But she was wrong. *Second, she assumed that her own sin somehow caused her son's death.* But that does not appear to be correct in this instance. *Third, she blamed Elijah.* It's human to find someone to blame when tragedy strikes.

The Prophet's Faith

As I read the text, a question comes to mind that I cannot answer. When the child first became ill, where was Elijah? Was he there, and did he pray for the boy? I assume the answer is yes, but the Bible doesn't tell us. I have a further question. When the child died, why did Elijah do what he did? Here's the answer. *He got involved because he saw God in everything, including all the sorrows of life.* I find his response instructive when the mother accuses him of coming to her house just to kill her son.

1. He doesn't get angry.
2. He doesn't try to explain why her son died.

3. He doesn't argue with her.
4. He doesn't make any excuses.

Instead he responds with incredible gentleness. Consider the words of F. B. Meyer: "If the Holy Spirit is really filling the heart, there will come over the rudest, the least refined, the most selfish person a marvelous change. There will be a gentleness in speech, a softness of the voice, a tender thoughtfulness in the smallest actions, an expression of abiding peace on the face. These shall be the evident seal of the Holy Ghost, the mint-mark of heaven. Are they evident in ourselves?"[1]

When the widow made her unkind accusation, Elijah responded simply. All he said is, "Give me your son" (v. 19a). When I go to visit a family where a death has occurred, I don't say as much as I used to. In my earlier years I would often do lots of talking. Looking back, I think I felt nervous and awkward, and I think I felt a need to try to explain things. I don't say much anymore. For one thing, I find that people in sorrow don't remember much that you say anyway, and there is always a danger of saying too much.

"He took him from her arms, carried him to the upper room where he was staying, and laid him on his bed. Then he cried out to the LORD, 'O LORD my God, have you brought tragedy also upon this widow I am staying with, by causing her son to die?' Then he stretched himself out on the boy three times and cried to the LORD, 'O LORD my God, let this boy's life return to him!'" (1 Kings 17:19a–21 NIV).

There is no easy way to explain what happens next. Elijah lies down on top of the body of the child. Foot to foot. Leg to leg. Chest to chest. Arm to arm. Hand to hand. Face to face. He does it not once, not twice, but three times. No one really knows exactly why he lay down even once, much less why he did it twice or three times. *Perhaps Elijah understood that to do anything for this boy he was going to have to get personally involved.* As a side note, since the boy was dead, he was now unclean under Jewish law. It was wrong for a prophet of God to touch a dead body, but extreme cases call for extreme measures. And so by lying down on the body of the child, it is as if he were saying, "Oh Lord, take some of the life from within me and give it to this boy." He prayed for a miracle because he believed in a power greater than death.

A. W. Pink pointed out seven noteworthy features of Elijah's prayer:

1. He went to his private room where he could be alone with God.
2. He prayed fervently.
3. He relied on his personal experience, calling him "My God."
4. He recalled God's sovereignty in causing this child to die.
5. He prayed earnestly and persistently.
6. He appealed to God's tender mercy toward this poor widow.
7. He made a definite request: "Let this boy's life return to him."[2]

Where did he learn to pray like that? Where is the precedent in the Bible prior to Elijah for anybody praying that way? Before this moment no one had ever been brought back from the dead. Enoch walked with God and was taken directly into heaven without dying. Moses died, and they never found his burial site. But that doesn't mean he was raised from the dead. This is the first case in biblical history of anyone who died and came back to life.

Where did he get faith to pray like this? It's not as if he could look back and say, "O God, as you did in the days of Moses," because God didn't do that in the days of Moses. He couldn't say, "O God, as you did for my father Abraham," because he didn't do anything like this in the days of Abraham. When Abraham offered Isaac, he regarded his son as being as good as dead, but that's not the same thing as actually dying. Nothing like this had ever happened before.

When Elijah prayed, he submitted himself completely to God. In himself the prophet had no power to bring this child back to life. He doesn't demand anything from the Lord, nor does he "name it and claim it." He humbly asks God to "let this boy's life return to him." That was as much as he could do. The rest was up to God.

God's Response

Now we see how God responds to Elijah's boiling prayer. "The Lord heard Elijah's cry" (v. 22). I love that. The text does not say the Lord heard Elijah's prayer, though he prayed. It says, "The Lord heard Elijah's cry." Have you ever wondered what the Bible means when it talks about how the Holy Spirit intercedes for us with groanings that cannot be uttered (Rom. 8:26–27)? When I lived in Southern California many years ago, I heard a Bible teacher tell of a wreck in which his wife was badly hurt. When he got to the crash scene, his wife was unconscious, and her life was hanging in the balance. As he rode in the ambulance to the hospital with her, this man stretched his arms over her body. "In that moment all I could do was say, 'O God, O Jesus, O God, O Jesus, O God, O Jesus.'" Then he added, "I felt like it was the first time in my life I had ever really prayed."

When I heard him say that, my mind went back to the night our first child was born. My wife was several weeks overdue, and that night there were various complications and difficulties. During the long hours of waiting, the doctor warned us that they might have to do a Caesarean delivery. Sometime in the late-night hours, the doctor came in and told us that the baby was having fetal heart distress. He showed us on the monitor how his heartbeat was going way up and way down. "We're going to watch this, but it doesn't look good."

Two or three hours passed, and about 5:15 in the morning—I'll never forget this—the doctor came striding in with a concerned look on his face. He spoke one sentence. "We're going to take the baby now." That was not a question. He wasn't asking for my permission. Suddenly the room exploded with activity. Nurses coming in and out, carts being wheeled in, someone grabbed my wife, and within thirty seconds the room was completely empty except for me. It happened so fast I didn't have a chance to kiss my wife good-bye. I didn't have a chance to pray with her. I didn't have a chance to do anything. The last thing I saw was the frightened face of my wife as they wheeled her into the delivery room. It was clear something bad was going on, and they were going to take the baby quickly. As I sat alone in that room, I tried to pray, but I couldn't. No words came out. All I could do was say, "Oh God, have mercy. Oh Jesus, have mercy. Oh God. Oh God."

After what seemed like seven hours, though it was only about twenty minutes later, the doctor came in and said, "Mr. Pritchard, you've got a son. He's healthy. He's going to be OK. Your wife is doing fine." And I felt that day like it was the first time I had ever prayed in my life.

Boiling Prayers

James 5:17 says Elijah was a man with a nature like ours. He had the same fears, the same doubts, the same worries, and the same concerns. The previous verse in the King James Version says that the effectual, fervent prayer of a righteous man avails much. The word *fervent* comes from a Greek word that means "boiling." *The boiling prayers of the righteous avail much with God.* What's a boiling prayer? It has nothing to do with standing or sitting, kneeling or lying down. It has nothing to do with lifting your voice or speaking in a whisper. It has nothing to do with how loud or how long you pray. I really don't need to define it all. When they take your son or daughter away for surgery, you'll discover what a boiling prayer is. When your children are in trouble, you'll pray boiling prayers to God. It's what happens when you pray like nothing else in the world really matters.

When the Bible says, "The LORD heard Elijah's cry" (1 Kings 17:22), it means that when he stretched himself out on that boy's dead body, something happened. God spoke from heaven and said, "All right, man of God, it shall be done." The application is simple. Pray like that, and you will see heaven opened on your behalf. The effective boiling prayer of the righteous avails much.

The boy's life returned to him and he lived. That boy who was dead came back to life. It's a pure miracle of God.

A Mother's Testimony

We come now to the end of this amazing story. Seeing that her son has come back to life, the grateful mother declares to Elijah, "Now I know that you are a man of God and that the word of the

LORD from your mouth is the truth" (1 Kings 17:24). The Bible doesn't record that she said, "Thank you," though surely she did. It's not recorded here because that's not the point. *Her words explain the miracle, and they also explain why not every mother receives this miracle when a child is sick to the point of death.* The miracle happened to authenticate Elijah as God's anointed prophet. God had promised to sustain all three of them—mother, son, and Elijah—until the rains came and drought ended (v. 14). On the basis of that promise, Elijah believed that God would bring the boy back to life. Strange as it may sound, the miracle is less about the boy and more about God's power working through Elijah. It is a miracle of sovereign grace, given this one time in Elijah's life and never again given during his ministry. God answered *this* prayer by *this* man in *this* way at *this* particular moment in time. And he did it for his own purposes. There is no other way to understand the story. This is a lesson about the Sovereign of the universe moving in a miraculous way in answer to the prophet's fervent prayers.

"Now I know," the widow says. Ponder those words. Think about what they mean. Here is a message from God for the church of Jesus Christ. The world waits to see the power of God. The world doesn't need another formula, and it certainly doesn't need more empty promises. The world needs what this woman needed—a demonstration of the power of the living God.

When John the Baptist was in prison, discouraged and besieged with doubt, he sent messengers to Jesus with this question: "Are you the One we've been waiting for, or should we look for someone else?" That's the right question. The world looks at us and says, "You talk a lot about Jesus, but how do we know he is the one we're looking for?" Remember that John had already called Jesus the Lamb of God who takes away the sin of the world (John 1:29). But now he says, "Are you the One, or should we look for someone else?" And what answer did Jesus give? He didn't rebuke John for his spiritual confusion, and he didn't quote Old Testament prophecy (which he could have done). Instead he instructed the messengers to go back and tell John what they had seen and heard. The blind see. The deaf hear. The lepers are cleansed. The lame walk. The dead are raised. And the poor have the gospel preached unto them (Matt. 11:1–6). Let the power of God be seen, and the world will pay attention to our message. Unbelievers ignore us because we have given them formulas when we need to demonstrate the power of the living God.

"Now I know," she says. Compare that with verse 18 where she speaks bitterly to Elijah. *Her bitterness turns to faith as she comes to understand that God only wounds in order to heal.* When the child is raised to life, the widow is encouraged, and the prophet is affirmed.

In our journey through Elijah's life, we have come to the end of the period of his personal preparation. Little does he know that he will soon confront the prophets of Baal in the greatest public showdown of his life. Before we go on, let's look at Elijah's preparation in perspective. Think of it this way:

> He lived in the ravine when he attended Dry Brook
> University.
> Then he moved on to Empty Barrel Graduate
> School.
> Now he has finished an internship at Resurrection
> Hospital.

All these things were part of Elijah's training to make him ready for the work God has for him to do. What did he learn from these three episodes?

At the brook he learned, "God can take care of me."

From the empty barrel he learned, "God can use me to help others."

From the child that died he learned, "God can work through me to do the impossible."

It's not by chance that in verse 1 of 1 Kings 17 he is called "Elijah the Tishbite," but in verse 24 the woman calls him a "man of God." God's preparation is finished. Elijah is now ready for the ultimate challenge. *No one becomes a man of God by chance, and no one becomes a man of God overnight.*

It's all about him.

It's not about us.

God must bring us to the end of ourselves so that we will learn that truth. Once we figure that out, we are ready to be used by God in a mighty way.

Chapter 6

OBADIAH: A GOOD MAN IN A HARD PLACE

"Drinking beer is easy. Trashing your hotel room is easy. But being a Christian, that's a tough call. That's rebellion."
ALICE COOPER

Ahab was angry, and that wasn't good news.

It wasn't just that he was having a bad day or a bad week or even a bad month. For Ahab things had gone bad for the last three years. That's a long stretch of bad luck, and it was bound to make a man grouchy, nervous, tense, upset, uptight, irritable, frustrated, and prone to losing his temper. You didn't want to be around the king when he was in a bad mood, which was most of the time.

Thoughtful observers of the court could pinpoint the exact moment when things began to go south. It happened the day that a strange man named Elijah came to the king's court in Samaria.

The man they called a prophet of the living God had declared that there would be no more rain or dew in Israel. It wasn't a long speech. In fact, no one could remember anyone ever making a shorter speech to the king. And it wasn't as if Elijah had been scared. If anything, he seemed almost eerily calm, as if he wasn't afraid of anything the king could do to him. This strange man from the mountains of Gilead had walked in, delivered his one-sentence message, and then he suddenly disappeared.

Elijah's Disappearing Act

It was the disappearing part that got to Ahab. That plus the drought and the famine. After Elijah vanished into thin air (or so it seemed), he evidently took the rain with him because just like that, the weather report for Samaria was always the same: clear skies, plenty of sun, no clouds, and no rain. Thus it had been for over three years.

The first few months had not been hard because you could always find some food and a bit of water if you knew where to look. But as the days passed, the storehouses emptied, the streams dried up, and a man with a bucket of water possessed a commodity more precious than gold. Soon the reports filtered in of crops that would not grow, of fields turning brown, of ground turned hard, of donkeys collapsing and cows that gave no milk. Slowly the poor began to starve to death. The king had to do something.

But what?

No wonder he was angry and upset. He was the most powerful man in Israel (or so he thought), and yet he was helpless to stop the drought. No matter how many prayers he offered to Baal, the heavens were shut up, and the rain would not come. To make matters much worse, Elijah had disappeared. Vanished with the wind. No one knew where he was, no one had seen him since that fateful day when he spoke his one-sentence message from God.

Where had he gone?

The king had stopped at nothing to answer that question. That's why he sent soldiers on a manhunt to the surrounding nations. In his frenzied paranoia to capture Elijah, he not only searched in other countries; he made their leaders swear they didn't know where the prophet was. But try as he might, he couldn't find the mountain man who brought drought and famine to his land. Evidently it never occurred to him to search the ravines east of the Jordan, and somehow Elijah escaped notice while living with the widow in Zarephath.

Now at last the word of the Lord came to Elijah again. "Go and present yourself to Ahab, and I will send rain on the land" (1 Kings 18:1 NIV). It must have come as a relief to Elijah to know that the time had come to confront the wicked king once again. Elijah was preeminently a man of action, and I do not doubt that many nights he must have wondered why he was languishing by the brook and in the widow's home while a tide of wickedness swept over his homeland. Surely he must have prayed and asked the Lord to do something. Perhaps he dreamed up various plans and strategies, but whatever he thought and however he prayed, it is entirely to Elijah's credit that he did nothing until God gave him the green light.

We all understand it is difficult for men of action to be removed from the spotlight. Fortune favors the bold, and the world bends to the man who does not sit and wait but seizes the tide. *Carpe diem!* Seize the day! Surely there was more than a little of this in Elijah's bold, fiery nature. Yet when sent into obscurity by the Lord, he instantly and uncomplainingly obeyed. How few there are who would do that today. The spotlight beckons, and we come running. But not Elijah. He waited until God's time had ripened, until the fullness of God's purposes could be revealed. Only then did he go in search of Ahab.

Elijah, Meet Obadiah

But it was not Ahab that he met. As he journeyed from Zarepath to Samaria, Elijah met Obadiah, who was in charge of Ahab's palace. In modern terms we would say he was Ahab's chief of staff, his right-hand man, the one who kept everything running smoothly. He took care of all the details so that Ahab could busy himself being king of Israel. If you stop to think about it, Obadiah must have been a man of considerable talent because this was a position with enormous responsibility. Obadiah was in charge of everything that happened in the palace. He had oversight of all the servants, the waiters, the helpers, and all the people who came in and out to see the king. *This certainly meant that Ahab must have known him well and placed a great deal of trust in him.* Get the wrong person in such a position, and your reign might be short. Find the right person, and your life suddenly becomes a lot easier. We all understand that there is the man who sits on the throne, and there is the man behind the throne who makes it all happen. The man on the throne gets the publicity, but it's the unseen man who deserves the credit. That was Obadiah.

Precisely at this point the story becomes fascinating because the Bible tells us two different and seemingly contradictory facts:

1. Ahab was a wicked man who did more evil than all the kings that preceded him.
2. Obadiah was a godly man who feared the Lord from his youth.

How did it come to pass that a godly man should be in charge of the palace for such a wicked man? We do not know the answer because the Bible tells us nothing about Obadiah's family background. This is what we know about Obadiah:

1. He was a devout believer in the Lord (v. 3).
2. He feared the Lord from his youth (v. 12).
3. He hid one hundred prophets of the Lord in a cave to keep Jezebel from killing them (v. 4).
4. He also supplied those prophets with food and water to keep them alive (v. 4).

Obadiah has been described as a "palm in the desert" because he stood for the Lord in a time of great national apostasy. When others were turning to idolatry, this man, elevated to a high position, would not bow the knee to Baal. He somehow managed to serve the Lord and to keep his high position even while serving a king bent on leading the people into a spiritual free fall.

Meyer versus Spurgeon

As I have studied the commentators, I find them divided in their evaluation of his character. F. B. Meyer sees him as a symbol of a believer caught in spiritual compromise: "Obadiah did not believe in carrying matters too far. Of course he could not fall in with this new order of things, but then there was no need for him to force his religious notions on everyone. He was often shocked at what he saw at court and found it hard to keep still, but then it was no business of his, and it would not do to throw up his situation, for he would be sure to lose it if he spoke out."[1]

I must say that I find those words somewhat unfair and see nothing in the text to substantiate them. I find myself more in agreement with Charles Spurgeon, who called Obadiah an example of "Early, Eminent Piety." He means that God ordained that Obadiah be raised in the fear of the Lord from his youth. And then it pleased the Lord to place this godly man in a position that must have been difficult for him, serving a wicked man like Ahab. Spurgeon also makes a point that, while it cannot be proved, makes sense to me. *He suggests that Elijah probably didn't have much patience with Obadiah's hesitation.* When Elijah told him to go tell Ahab where he (Elijah) was, Obadiah was plainly afraid to go. He thought it was a virtual death sentence for himself because all he knew was that Elijah had shown up at the king's courts three years earlier and then suddenly disappeared without a trace. And now Elijah shows up again. If Obadiah goes to the king and says, "I've found Elijah," how does he know that Elijah won't disappear again? To me that's a perfectly logical question. Obadiah was counting the cost before opening his mouth, something Jesus himself advised us to do. I think it is clear that Obadiah doesn't mind dying for what he believes, but he doesn't want to be killed for no reason at all.

Serving Christ in the Air Force

Following Christ doesn't mean giving up your common sense. When believers in China worship behind closed doors, is it wrong to close the curtains so as not to draw attention to your meeting? Is this not what Jesus meant when he told his disciples to be wise as serpents but harmless as doves? And what about the biblical injunction to walk circumspectly, which means to walk with your eyes wide open, looking around you at all times?

I had the privilege of spending several hours with an exceptional young man who serves as a second lieutenant in the air force. He has just written a book calling single men to moral purity. When I asked him how others feel about his strong faith, he told me that he had thought about it a lot and had asked other Christians in the air force who had served a long time how they balanced their faith and their military careers. His answer boiled down to this. *The best way to serve Christ in the military is to do your job with excellence every single day.* He said he doesn't have to talk about his faith overtly because by serving well, others notice what he does and eventually doors open for conversations about the Lord. It isn't profitable to make a public show about his faith because that only antagonizes other people. But it also became clear to me that here was a young man with rock-solid convictions who would not compromise just to get ahead in his career. He's young and just starting out, and I imagine that he will be put in some tough places where he'll have to think carefully about how to respond as a Christian. But so what? That's true of everyone who names the name of Christ. A godly high school principal has to think carefully about how much or how little to say about the Lord when he is on the job. A Christian judge has to balance the demands of his job with the convictions of his heart. It's the same for lawyers and pharmacists and teachers and businessmen and women and anyone who rubs shoulders with the people of the world. You will often find yourself in situations where you need the wisdom of Solomon to know how to respond without compromising your convictions. Sometimes you'll know what to do, and you have to find the courage to do the right thing. Occasionally you will have to do things that others will not understand.

How can anyone criticize Obadiah for hiding the prophets of the Lord from Jezebel? If he had been found out, surely she would have had him put to death on the spot. He knew that, and he hid them anyway, and he risked his life to give them food and water. Say what you will about the man, but Obadiah was no coward.

Let me go back to Spurgeon's point for just a moment. He begins his sermon this way: "I suspect that Elijah did not think very much of Obadiah. He does not treat him with any great consideration, but addresses him more sharply than one would expect from a fellow-believer. Elijah was the man of action—bold, always to the front, with nothing to conceal; Obadiah was a quiet believer, true and steadfast, but in a very difficult position, and therefore driven to perform his duty in a less open manner. His faith in the Lord swayed his life, but did not drive him out of the court."[2]

That makes good sense to me. Sometimes our eagerness to judge other believers stems less from spiritual insight and more from differences in personality. Elijah could never have served in Ahab's court. Never! Such a thought would have been abhorrent to him. Why would he, a prophet of God, serve in the court of a man given to such wickedness? But that was evidently exactly where God had placed Obadiah.

No Cookout for Them!

Elijah was a mountain man, not suited to the refined life of a king's court.

Obadiah had the training and temperament to serve the king well. He would not have survived long in the mountains of Gilead.

If Elijah didn't understand Obadiah, and if Obadiah feared Elijah, it is perfectly understandable. I don't think Obadiah would have invited Elijah over for a cookout, and if he had, I doubt that Elijah would have come. Many years ago I heard it explained this way. In the Lord's army there are prophets and there are priests. The prophets are called by God to speak boldly, rebuking sin and calling people to righteousness. The priests are called by God to see the hurting people all around them and to minister healing in Jesus' name. We see the dichotomy often in dealing with moral issues like abortion and gay rights. There are those who are called to denounce these sins, and there are those who are called to minister to those hurt and ruined by these sins. I have observed that the prophets rarely understand the priests, and the priests don't appreciate the prophets. Prophets often look at the priests as soft and weak, while the priests see the prophets as harsh and uncaring. But both are called by the Lord, and both have important jobs to do.

Someone has to speak out and take the heat.

Someone has to bind up the wounded.

Someone has to declare God's Word boldly.

Someone has to help the hurting.

Someone has to stand and fight.

Someone has to take care of the casualties.

The army can't be all fighters and no healers. And it can't be all healers and no fighters. You need both, and you need both at the same time even when they don't always see eye to eye.

It would be easy but simplistic for me to say, "Can't we all get along?" Sometimes we can; sometimes we can't. If we can't always work together, at least we can hold our convictions in love, understanding that not everyone is called to do what we are called to do. For every Elijah, there are a dozen Obadiahs. And the prophet needed Obadiah whether he knew it or not. For it was Obadiah who paved the way for the prophet to meet the king again.

Elijah Needs Obadiah

Thank God for every Elijah who stands in the gap, proclaiming God's truth without fear or favor. Thank God for every pastor who stands for righteousness and takes the heat for it and doesn't flinch. And God bless those pastors who go on Larry King and say the same thing on CNN that they say in their pulpits on Sunday morning. God bless them a thousand times for not backing down when they sit next to Deepak Chopra, who to his credit doesn't back down from his New Age nonsense. We might as well be at least as bold about our faith as the people of the world are about what they believe. So God bless Franklin Graham for saying on TV that Jesus is the only way to heaven. Let him go ahead and say it even if some people don't like it.

But Elijah isn't the whole story. *He can't do his job without Obadiah to help him. And there are more Obadiahs than Elijahs in the world.* God bless every Christian schoolteacher who prays for her students, who knows their names, and who strives to live for Christ while teaching in the public schools. God bless every Christian doctor and lawyer and every Christian businessman and woman who see their job as part of their calling from the Lord.

If you are an Elijah, do not despise Obadiah, who serves where you could not serve.

If you are Obadiah, do not reject Elijah, who does what you could not do.

We all have a job to do, and we will be happier in it if we realize that most everyone else we know will be doing something different. Our challenge is to do what we do with grace, courage, zeal, and humility, and leave the judging of others to the Lord. C. S. Lewis expressed this same truth in a more colorful way: "The work of a Beethoven, and the work of a charwoman, become spiritual on precisely the same condition, that of being offered to God, of being done humbly 'as to the Lord.' This does not, of course, mean that it is for anyone a mere toss-up whether he should sweep rooms or compose symphonies. A mole must dig to the glory of God and a cock must crow."[3]

Would it have been better for Obadiah to have resigned his position? Not necessarily.

Joseph served in Pharaoh's court.

Mordecai waited at Ahasuerus's gate.

Daniel served the pagan king Nebuchadnezzar.

Philippians 4:22 tells us there were "saints" in Caesar's household.

Bono, lead singer of the rock group U2, sums up his life this way: "I'm a musician. I write songs. I just hope when the day is done I've been able to tear a little corner off of the darkness."[4] That might be Obadiah's testimony also. By serving in Ahab's court, he kept the light of God shining when darkness had almost completely covered the land.

God has always placed his people in some unlikely places. And he sometimes calls others to do things that we ourselves simply could not do. If God has called them, he will supply them and give them whatever they need. To say this is not to make any allowance for spiritual compromise because if you compromise your principles, you would be better off not calling yourself a Christian at all. Those who serve Caesar (or some wicked boss) may find that they, too, must hide God's prophets at considerable risk to themselves. It's never easy to serve Jesus, and it's not getting any easier.

God has all sorts of people in his family. Elijah had a rough road from the beginning, but it wasn't easy to be in Obadiah's shoes either. Both men served the Lord, and in this case we stop to give a word of praise for Obadiah, a small link in the big chain of God's purposes.

Faithfulness counts with the Lord. Remember Obadiah, God's "palm in the desert." He was a good man in a hard place who did the right thing when it mattered most. God bless him, and God bless everyone who follows in his steps.

Chapter 7

*B*AAL BUSTER

"Let's roll."

TODD BEAMER, UNITED FLIGHT 93, SEPTEMBER 11, 2001

*I*t is sometimes said that a crisis never makes a man; it only reveals what he already is. That thought is both comforting and frightening because we all wonder how we would react if everything we held dear were really on the line.

Our family . . .

Our health . . .

Our career . . .

Our life . . .

We wonder, would we have the faith to make it? Or would we collapse? All the things we say we believe—would they still be enough when the crunch comes? We all wonder what we would do in that moment if everything we held dear were on the line. That's one reason we remember Todd Beamer. If you'd been on

United Flight 93 on 9/11, what would you have done? Would you have kept quiet, or would you have had the courage to say, "Are you ready? Let's roll." You put the phone down and join the others who are storming down the aisle toward your destiny. If everything we believed was coming down to one crystallized moment, if we had to decide where we really stood, if it was our family, our wife, our husband, our children, our job, if everything we held dear were on the line, would we have the courage, would we have the faith, would we have the fortitude, would we be there when it really counted? Whatever else you can say about Todd Beamer, September 11, 2001 didn't change him. It only revealed what was already there on the inside.

Certain stories in the Bible have become so well-known that when we mention the person's name, we automatically think of a particular event. When we say Noah, we think of the flood. We say Abraham, we think of Isaac. We say Joshua, we think of Jericho. When we say David, we think of Goliath. When we say Daniel, we think of the lions' den. When we say Elijah, we think of the crisis on Mount Carmel.

If you ever go to the Holy Land, your guide will take you to Carmel. It is an enormous mountain by the seacoast overlooking the modern-day city of Haifa. From the top of Mount Carmel you have a commanding view in all directions. Carmel was important in the Old Testament for military and geopolitical reasons. Whoever held Mount Carmel controlled the northern half of the nation. And whoever controlled the worship that took place on Carmel controlled the nation spiritually. The priests and the prophets of Baal knew that. That is why years earlier they had built an altar to Baal on top of Mount Carmel. We know from history that Baal worship was a particularly degrading religion. It was a bizarre mixture of idolatry, perverted sexuality, and child sacrifice. The pagans believed Baal controlled the rising and the setting of the sun. He was also considered the god who brought forth the seasons, the god who brought forth or withheld the rains. Because ancient Israel was an agricultural nation, Baal was an extremely powerful deity. Men and women who came to worship Baal would offer a sacrifice and then engage in some sort of sexual activity with the priests and priestesses. They believed that if you were joined physically to one of those priests or priestesses of Baal, the power of Baal would be transferred to you. Thus Baal worship appealed on one level to the mind, on another level to their economic well-being, and on a deeper level to the desires of the flesh.

We should therefore not be surprised that even in Israel, a nation dedicated to the one true God, Baal worship became extremely popular. It grabbed the mind, the heart, the body, and ultimately the soul. Under the reign of wicked king Ahab, Baal worship had virtually swept the Northern Kingdom. The worship of the one true God had been almost completely extinguished.

Here Comes Elijah

Against that backdrop we read the story of Elijah, a mountain man whose name means "the Lord is my God." One day without warning he appeared before Ahab, that wicked toad squatting on the throne of Israel. Elijah said to the king, "I have come to you in the name of the living God, the God of Israel, before whom I stand. And I tell you there shall be no rain in Israel and even no dew until I give the word." Having uttered those words by the power of Almighty God, Elijah was sent by the Lord to the brook

Cherith where he stayed in hiding for a while. Eventually the Lord moved him to Sidonian territory, to the widow of Zarephath where the Bible records the miracle of the flour and the oil that did not run out and the miracle of the raising of the widow's son. Meanwhile in the nation of Israel, the famine set in. For more than three years there had been no rain. The ground turned brown and began to crack. The creeks dried up, the brooks disappeared, and the Jordan River became little more than a trickle. All across the land the crops were dying on the vine. Animals became carcasses lying in the fields.

Finally God tapped Elijah on the shoulder and said, "Go see Ahab again." When the king and the prophet met the second time, the king asked, "Is that you, you troubler of Israel?" (1 Kings 18:17 NIV). The Hebrew word for *troubler* sometimes means "snake."[1] "You dirty snake." That's what the king thought of God's anointed prophet. Elijah turned the tables and said, "I have not made trouble for Israel. . . . But you and your father's family have. You have abandoned the LORD's commands and have followed the Baals" (v. 18 NIV). Before Ahab could say anything else, Elijah said, "It's time for the truth to come out. It's time for the people to decide." He said to the king, "Tell all the people of Israel to meet me at Carmel." That was agreeable to the king. Elijah said, "Send 450 prophets of Baal, and send 400 priests of Asherah," who was thought to be the female consort of Baal. That's 850 false prophets versus one man of God.

Asherah was a leading female deity in the Canaanite religion, considered to be the wife of El, the chief god. Commonly regarded as the goddess of fertility, she was worshipped at groves of evergreen trees or places marked by wooden poles. The Bible repeatedly warns against the worship of Asherah (Exod. 34:13; Deut. 7:5; Judg. 6:25; 2 Kings 23:4).

I pause to comment that either Elijah was crazy, or he was a man in touch with his God. You'd better not do that kind of thing on a whim or the spur of the moment. You'd better be sure you're in touch with the Lord. Elijah was a man who was in touch with Almighty God. On the appointed day they met on top of Mount Carmel. We pick up the story in verses 20–21. "So Ahab sent word throughout all Israel and assembled the prophets on Mount Carmel. Elijah went before the people and said, 'How long will you waver between two opinions? If the LORD is God, follow him; but if Baal is god, follow him'" (NIV). The most important part comes in the next sentence. "But the people said nothing." Of all the things that plague modern Christianity, perhaps this is the greatest. Spiritual indecision. Spiritual juggling. The inability of the people of God to make up our minds, to decide which side we're really on, the inability of young people and adults and singles and those who are married, the inability of every age and every group inside our churches to decide which team we're on. We can't decide who we're going to play for. And that's why we struggle about which uniform we're going to put on in the morning.

Note the little word *if*. The word *if* means you have to make up your mind. There is a time to think, and there is a time to decide. *If* the Lord is God. Is he or isn't he? Here is one of the reasons I love Elijah. *He made it practical and personal.* He did not say, "If the Lord is God, buy a book and think about it." He said, "If the Lord is God, get on his team and follow him. And if Baal is god, fine, then get on his team and follow him. But stop sitting on the fence. You've got to decide sooner or later."

Dorothy Sayers put the matter this way: "In the world it is called Tolerance, but in hell it is called Despair, the sin that believes in nothing, cares for nothing, seeks to know nothing, interferes with nothing, enjoys nothing, hates nothing, finds purpose in nothing, lives for nothing, and remains alive because there is nothing for which it will die."[2]

Tolerance has its place, but none when it comes to questions of ultimate truth. If everything is equally true, if we never have to choose, if everything is right, then nothing is really wrong, and we might as well support Baal or God or maybe we should just give up and watch TV because nothing really matters anyway. The line between tolerance and despair is thin indeed, and the people of Israel had long since crossed that line.

850 to 1

He proposed a simple experiment so the people would know which God was the true God. You can argue all day long about which soap gets you cleaner. If you really want to know, get in the water and take a bath and see who comes out cleaner. Elijah said, "You take Baal, and I'll take the Lord God of Israel. The one who answers by fire, he is God." We could use more of that sort of courage today. We need a little less talk and a lot more action. There comes a time when talk is cheap. The people of Israel were halting between two opinions. "We think maybe our God is God. Or maybe Baal is God. Maybe we can mix the two somehow." A little of this, a little of that. Elijah said, "No, now the time has come to make up your mind."

The story itself is simple. The prophets of Baal cut up a bull and laid the pieces on the wood, but Elijah would not let them set it on fire. "Ask Baal to light the fire for you." He told the prophets of Baal and Asherah to do whatever they thought they needed to do in order to entice Baal to send fire from heaven. In preparing this chapter, I read Alfred Edersheim's discussion of this passage. Much of his description of Baal worship sounds like voodoo. He says the prophets of Baal had hair down to their shoulders. When they danced, they would scream and beat their drums and lower their bodies almost to the ground. They bowed to the ground to show their devotion to Baal.[3] Remember that sexual immorality lay at the core of Baal worship. Don't imagine some sedate scene like a Wednesday night prayer meeting. Think of wild screaming and various sexualized antics up on the mountain. They carried on for hours, calling out, "O Baal, answer us. Answer us." Nothing happened. At noon Elijah began to taunt them. "Shout louder! . . . Surely he is a god! Perhaps he is deep in thought, or busy, or traveling. Maybe he is sleeping and must be awakened" (v. 27 NIV). This is very non-PC. Elijah is definitely not politically correct. We don't do this sort of thing anymore. We don't make fun of other people's religion. You get in trouble for doing that. If you did what Elijah did, you might be arrested for a hate crime.

When Elijah suggests that perhaps Baal is busy, he uses a Hebrew word that has a variety of meanings. Some say that the word means that he's gone off hunting. Others suggest it means to go to the bathroom. That's quite an insult if you think about it. Elijah is a mountain man. He's not afraid of embarrassing people. He'll say anything that comes to mind.

Toward the end of the afternoon, in desperation the prophets of Baal took knives and swords and began cutting themselves as a kind of blood sacrifice to their false god. How desperate they were. But the heavens were silent. Baal had utterly failed.

The Soaking Wet Sacrifice

Verse 30 is perhaps the most important verse in the chapter. "Then Elijah said to all the people, 'Come here to me.' They came to him, and he repaired the altar of the LORD, which was in ruins" (NIV). Taking twelve stones, one for each of the twelve tribes, he rebuilt the altar of the Lord. *This was a symbolic sign that the nation would now return to its true spiritual heritage.* The timing is also significant. Elijah rebuilt the altar late in the afternoon, about the time of the evening sacrifice. This was the time God had appointed, but Israel had completely forgotten about it. Now at the appointed hour for the evening sacrifice, he built the altar, dug a trench, and laid the wood in place. He cut up the bull, laid the pieces on the wood, and then told the people to soak the wood with four large jugs of water. Three times he ordered the water poured.

Until that bull is soaking wet.

Until the wood is soaking wet.

Until the altar is soaking wet.

Until there is so much water it fills the trench around the altar.

By doing these radical things at the time of the evening sacrifice, Elijah was saying, "Our God is a covenant God. If we come back to him according to his word, he will not turn us away. If we come back to him on his terms, in the right way at the right time, he will come through for us." Though the people had forgotten, God still was ready to keep his promise.

So at the hour of sacrifice, everything was ready. But they needed a miracle. So Elijah stepped forward and prayed a simple prayer: "O LORD, God of Abraham, Isaac and Israel, let it be known today that you are God in Israel and that I am your servant and have done all these things at your command. Answer me, O LORD, answer me, so these people will know that you, O LORD, are God, and that you are turning their hearts back again" (vv. 36–37 NIV). On one side you have 850 prophets of Baal and Asherah; and you have eight, nine, ten hours of screaming and yelling and whooping and cutting themselves; and you have all their prayers to their fake God. You have all that religiosity. And over here you have one man, the mountain man, God's man. When he prays, he uses only sixty words in English. He prays for three things:

> Lord, answer me so they'll know you are the true God.
>
> Answer me so they will know that I am your prophet and doing your will.
>
> Answer me so that the hearts of the people may be turned back to you.

Elijah's only concern was for God, his word, his work, his glory, and God's people. Lord, answer me. No screaming. No whooping. No hollering. No cutting themselves. I am impressed by the simple dignity of it all.

By the way, the water wasn't necessary. *God could answer without the water.* God could answer in a rainstorm. God could answer in a snowstorm. God could answer at the bottom of a well. That wasn't any problem for God. The water was just to convince the people that it was no trick, that it was the Lord God himself who answered. The point of this whole story is really not about Elijah. And the point of the story is really not about the people, and the point of the story surely isn't about Ahab and the prophets of Baal. They're just window dressing. *This is a story about God.* It is not about Elijah. He's just the instrument through whom God works an incredible miracle.

When God answers, he answers completely so there could never be any doubt:

> The fire consumed the sacrifice.
> The fire consumed the wood beneath the sacrifice.
> The fire consumed the water in the trench.
> The fire consumed the rocks of the altar.

Scoreboard!

Let's go over it one final time to make sure we've got the point.

850 prophets of Baal and Asherah versus Elijah

850 to 1

Doesn't sound like a fair fight.

Scoreboard!

Elijah 10,000,000

Prophets of Baal 0

Oops! I made a mistake in that calculation. It should be . . .

850 to 1 plus God!

It's not a fair fight. The bad guys needed a lot more help on their side. But it still wouldn't have been a fair fight.

As the story comes to an end, three things happen:

1. The people finally wake up, their eyes are opened, they fall down and cry out, "The Lord, he is God; the Lord, he is God."

2. The people seize the prophets of Baal. Elijah had them brought to the Kishon Valley where they were slaughtered. That may sound unkind, but was it? I don't think so. Husbands, let's suppose the doctor tells you that your wife has breast cancer.

Let's further suppose that she needs an operation. After it's over, the doctor says, "She's OK, and the operation was successful." You're going to ask him one question. "Did you get it all?" That's really the only thing that matters. Did you get it all? The prophets of Baal were a spiritually malignant tumor inside the body of the people of God. Elijah was going to get them all! He wasn't going to leave any part of that tumor inside the body of the nation of Israel.

Edersheim paints a vivid picture of that moment: "And so Israel was once more converted unto God. And now, in accordance with the Divine command in the Law (Deuteronomy 13:13; 17:2, etc.), stern judgment must be executed on the idolaters and seducers, the idol-priests. The victory that day must be complete; the renunciation of Baal-worship beyond recall. Not one of the priests of Baal must escape. Down the steep mountain sides they hurried them, cast them over precipices, those fourteen hundred feet to the river Kishon, which was reddened with their blood."[4]

3. It started to rain. Seven times Elijah sent his servant to look toward the sea. Six times the servant saw nothing, but the seventh time he saw a cloud about the size of a man's hand. When the rain started, Ahab retreated to his summer palace in Jezreel. Here is the final verse of the story: "The power of the LORD came upon Elijah and, tucking his cloak into his belt, he ran ahead of Ahab all the way" (v. 46 NIV).

Three Frogs on a Log

As we wrap up, let's go back to the beginning, to the words Elijah spoke to the people of Israel: "Choose you this day whom you will serve. If God be God, follow him; if Baal be god, follow him" (see v. 21). And the people did nothing, which is the great problem today inside the church. At some point you've got to make up your mind.

Let me ask a simple question. Three frogs are sitting on a log. Two decide to jump off. How many are left? The answer is three. You haven't jumped off the log because you decided to jump off. Deciding counts for nothing. *You're still on the log until you jump off the log.* You can decide till the cows come home, but as long as you're sitting on the log, you're still sitting on the log. You can say I have decided to follow Jesus. You can sing it. You can shout it. But until you're following him, you're not following him. I don't care what you decided. It's not your decisions that matter; it's what you actually do.

Let me wrap up this chapter by asking a personal question: *What is it that keeps you from being a wholehearted follower of Jesus Christ?* Is it your social life? Many young people and many singles struggle at precisely this point. You want to be where the action is, and you fear that if you follow Jesus, you'll miss out on the action of life. A young woman sent me an e-mail describing her own spiritual dilemma. For years she had struggled with being "two different people"—one person at church and another person during the week. This is part of what she wrote: "For years I've gone out to have drinks with friends, often, and have made the worst choices in my life as a result of some of those nights . . . and then I turn around and rely on church to make me feel whole again. It's been an endless cycle, and as of yesterday, it's done. I realize that I can't combine the two lifestyles, that I have to choose one, and the choice is obvious."

She went on to say that she knows she will still have struggles and that the devil is ticked off that she has decided to follow Christ. *She's right on both counts.* Just as I wrote those words, I recalled an incident from the early days of evangelist D. L. Moody. On his first trip to Great Britain, before he had become well-known, Moody was introduced to someone who asked the one making the introduction, "Is he O and O?" That meant, Is he out and out for Jesus? The answer was a definite yes. Suppose someone were to ask, "Are you O and O?" How would you answer? Perhaps a better question would be, how would your friends answer that question about you? Is your walk so clear and your commitment so strong that everyone around you knows that you are O and O for Jesus?

At some point if we are Christians we must take the advice of Flannery O'Connor: "Push back against the age as hard as it pushes against you. What people don't realize is how much religion costs. They think faith is a big electric blanket, when of course it is the cross."[5]

Let me challenge you with the words of Elijah put in a contemporary context: *If Jesus Christ be God, follow him! If anything else or anyone else be God, follow him!* But make up your mind. Stop playing games. Stop your spiritual juggling. Stop working both sides of the street. Stop sitting on the fence. Take your stand for what you know to be true.

Some of you reading my words have been like a child standing by the edge of the pool, sticking your toe in the edge of the water, checking to see how deep it is. It's fine to check the water. You ought to do that. It's the smart thing to do. But at some point you've got to jump in the water.

Are you ready to jump in? Are you ready to go O and O for Jesus? I challenge you to stop what you are doing and get on your knees and talk to the Lord. It's time to stop thinking about planning to someday soon make a full commitment of your life to Jesus Christ. Do it now!

How long will you try to be two different people? It's time to say, "All in," time to become O and O for Jesus.

Now is the time.

No more delays.

No more excuses.

It's time to make up your mind.

Chapter 8

ROPHET ON THE RUN

"Everyone has a game plan until they get hit in the mouth."
MIKE TYSON

*O*ne of the reasons we know the Bible is the Word of God is because it doesn't sugarcoat the truth about its heroes. When the Bible tells us about great men and great women, it does not give us just the good news; it also gives us the bad news. When the Bible describes the great heroes of the Old Testament and the New Testament, it tells us the unvarnished truth about their struggles, their temptations, their difficulties, and their defeats.

- When the Bible tells us about Noah who built an ark, it also tells us how Noah got drunk and was exposed before his sons.
- When the Bible tells us the story of Abraham, the great father of the faith, it also tells us how not once but twice he lied about his wife Sarah in order to save his own skin.

- When the Bible tells us about Jacob, it tells us not only about his great exploits of faith, it also tells us about how he cheated his brother Esau and how he cheated others during his lifetime.
- When the Bible tells us the story of Moses, it doesn't just tell us about the parting of the Red Sea. It also tells us how Moses murdered the Egyptian, and it also tells us how he struck the rock in defiance of the Lord's command and was denied entrance into the promised land.
- When the Bible tells us about David, it doesn't just tell us about his great victory over Goliath; it also tells us about his adultery and his murder of Uriah the Hittite.
- When the Bible tells us about Peter, it doesn't just tell us about how he walked on water; it also tells us about that dark night in which he not once, not twice, but three times denied the Lord.

When the Bible paints the picture of its great heroes, it does not just use the light colors of victory and happiness and joy. It also paints the full portrait with the dark colors of sadness, difficulty, depression, defeat, sin, and temptation. That is certainly the case when we come to the story of that great mountain man Elijah. When last we visited our hero, he had won his great victory over Ahab and the prophets of Baal at Mount Carmel. *Immediately the story moves from his greatest victory to his most humiliating defeat.* Without a pause we go from the top to the bottom. This is the story of Elijah's battle with discouragement, despondency, and depression. One writer calls this "Elijah's nervous breakdown." I do not doubt that that is a good description.

The Thrill of Victory, the Agony of Defeat

And I remind you again of what has just happened. Elijah has been up on the mountain where he faced down the 850 prophets of Baal. It was 850 to one. The prophets of Baal danced around and moaned and groaned and put their long hair down on the ground, and they prophesied to Baal, and they cut themselves, and nothing happened. Then Elijah prayed a simple prayer asking God to demonstrate his mighty power that the hearts of the people might be turned back to the Lord. Immediately fire from heaven came down, consuming not only the offering on the altar but also licking up all the water that was in the trench. The people of Israel bowed down and said, "The Lord, he is God; the Lord, he is God." All the prophets of Baal were slaughtered. An enormous thunderstorm came in from the ocean, drenching the land and breaking the drought. The story ends with Ahab heading back to Jezreel to bring the bad news to Jezebel. But Elijah was so pumped up that he outran Ahab's chariot. You would think that the next chapter might begin this way: *"And Elijah rejoiced in the Lord his God. He made a sacrifice to give thanks to God, and all the people came to Elijah, and he preached unto them the word of the Lord."* That's not what happens. Elijah ends up a long way away from Jezreel. He heads south down to Beersheba. He heads south and west far out of the land of promise back down to Mount Horeb, which is another name for Mount Sinai. Hundreds of miles away, he holes up in a cave and prays for God to take his life. This is the story of Elijah's battle with depression.

We all understand that depression is a major problem in our time. Every year in America 9.5 percent of all adults are diagnosed with some degree of clinical depression. Experts tell us that one out of every four women will suffer from clinical depression at some point and one out of every ten men. Researchers attribute that difference in numbers to the fact that men are far less likely to admit their problems and far less likely to seek help. Depression costs American companies $44 billion a year. It is the leading cause of disability in America. We know that there are many causes for depression, and these things are often interrelated, including stress, difficulty in personal relationships, medical problems, poor diet, trauma, and genetic factors. Symptoms include persistent sadness, feelings of hopelessness, loss of energy, difficulty concentrating, sleeplessness, and irritability, and sometimes it may lead to thoughts of suicide. Researchers tell us that depression seems to be spread across all sectors of society. No one is exempt, and it's not a matter of IQ, age, or social class. Some of the greatest people in history have struggled with feelings of depression. Who said this? "I am now the most miserable man living. If what I feel were distributed to the whole human family, there would not be one cheerful face on earth. . . . To remain as I am is impossible. I must die to be better."[1]

Ever felt that way? "I must die to be better." Abraham Lincoln felt that way because those were his words.

The Minister's Fainting Fits

Many people consider Charles Haddon Spurgeon, the famous London pastor of the late 1800s, to be the greatest preacher since the apostle Paul. Yet Spurgeon openly admitted that he often struggled with depression. It is a matter of record that Spurgeon, who lived with various physical maladies, on more than one occasion was so overcome with feelings of worthlessness, depression, and despondency that he left his pulpit in London to go to a resort in France where he stayed for two or three months at a time. Often he spent days resting on the couch because he was so depressed, so fearful, and so despondent. His marvelous book *Lectures to My Students* contains a chapter called "The Minister's Fainting Fits," which Warren Wiersbe says every pastor should read at least once a year because Spurgeon is so honest about the pressures that men and women in the ministry face. He begins his chapter this way:

> As it is recorded that David, in the heat of battle, waxed faint, so may it be written of all the servants of the Lord. Fits of depression come over the most of us. Usually cheerful as we may be, we must at intervals be cast down. The strong are not always vigorous, the wise not always ready, the brave not always courageous, and the joyous not always happy. There may be here and there men of iron, to whom wear and tear work no perceptible detriment, but surely the rust frets even these; and as for ordinary men, the Lord knows, and makes them to know, that they are but dust. Knowing by most painful experience what deep depression of spirit means, being visited therewith at seasons by no means few or far between, I thought it might be consolatory to some of my brethren if I gave my thoughts thereon, that younger men might not fancy that some strange thing had happened to them when they became for a season possessed by melancholy; and that sadder men might know that one upon whom the sun has shone right joyously did not always walk in the light.[2]

He goes on to say many helpful things in the chapter, but one point seems especially relevant. In giving a list of the times when we are most prone to depression, this is where he begins: "First among them I must mention *the hour of great success*. When at last a long-cherished desire is fulfilled, when God has been glorified greatly by our means, and a great triumph achieved, then we are apt to faint. It might be imagined that amid special favors our soul would soar to heights of ecstasy, and rejoice with joy unspeakable, but it is generally the reverse. The Lord seldom exposes his warriors to the perils of exultation over victory; he knows that few of them can endure such a test, and therefore dashes their cup with bitterness."[3]

He offers Elijah as proof of this point and concludes that in some measure depression and discouragement after a great victory are part of the gracious discipline of God's mercy lest we become proud and puffed up at our own accomplishments. In that light we should study this ancient story, for it has much to teach us today. *The Bible records this story for the benefit of all who serve the Lord.* What happened to Spurgeon, what happened to Lincoln, what happened to Elijah will probably happen to all of us sooner or later.

His Condition Examined

The story begins this way: "Now Ahab told Jezebel everything Elijah had done and how he had killed all the prophets with the sword. So Jezebel sent a messenger to Elijah to say, 'May the gods deal with me, be it ever so severely, if by this time tomorrow I do not make your life like that of one of them'" (1 Kings 19:1–2 NIV). You can just imagine with what eagerness

Jezebel, that evil shrew, waited for the return of her husband Ahab. When she saw his chariot returning from Mount Carmel, she assumed it must be with good news. When he came into the palace at Jezreel, I am sure his face was ashen.

No doubt she asked him what happened on the mountain. Since it was raining across the land, I suppose Jezebel took it as a sign that the prophets of Baal had won the day. Ahab gave her the bad news.

"What happened to the prophets of Baal?"

"They're all dead."

"What happened on top of the mountain?"

"The Lord God of Elijah won the day, and Baal was defeated."

Shakespeare said that hell hath no fury like a woman scorned. Now Jezebel was going to get even. She sent a messenger to Elijah with some ominous news: "May the gods deal with me, be it ever so severely, if by this time tomorrow . . ." (v. 2 NIV). I think it's the *tomorrow* part that got to Elijah. He was not a man who would have gotten easily flustered by a nonspecific threat. Jezebel is saying, "Check your watch, man of God, because by this time tomorrow, I'm going to slice you and dice you the same way you did to the prophets of Baal."

How did Elijah respond? *First, he was gripped by fear and doubt (v. 3)*. Why be afraid of this woman? Elijah just saw God do a miracle. He helped slaughter the false prophets.

Second, he reacted impulsively. The text says that he ran from Jezreel, which is in the northern part of Israel, not far from the Sea of Galilee, all the way to Beersheba, the far southern border of the nation. He ran south past Jerusalem, past Bethlehem, past Hebron. Elijah was so scared that he decided to run as far from

Jezebel as he could get. That meant a change in climate because Jezreel is pastureland, but in Beersheba he was in the desert.

Third, he wanted to be alone. "When he came to Beersheba in Judah, he left his servant there" (v. 3 NIV). That was a big mistake. *The one thing he most needed was somebody to encourage him.* Leaving his servant in Beersheba, he ventured into the desert a day's journey, sat under a broom tree, and prayed that he might die. Elijah was on his way to the most remote place he could find. When you're gripped by fear and doubt, you want to run away and be by yourself.

Fourth, he allowed himself to be controlled by dark thoughts. Ever felt this way? "Lord, I've had enough. Lord, this is it. Take my life. I am a total failure." At this moment mighty Elijah, God's mountain man, was filled with self-pity. Having temporarily lost his faith in God and being gripped by fear and doubt, he ran away from his problems. Overwhelmed by despair, he was filled with dark thoughts. This can happen to any of us. Have you ever taken one of those stress tests where they allot points for traumatic events in your life? If we gave Elijah that test, he would be off the charts. Before you get down on him, walk a mile in his shoes. He didn't respond rightly to the pressure he faced, but how many of us would have done any better?

Can you think of anybody in the New Testament who temporarily lost his faith and his bearings? Can you think of anybody in prison who couldn't remember what he had known earlier to be true? Consider John the Baptist. When he saw Jesus walking toward him, he cried out, "Look, the Lamb of God, who takes away the sin of the world!" (John 1:29 NIV). Later Herod had John put into prison where he was ultimately beheaded. Those of us who have never been behind bars don't understand what prison is like. There is no place on earth darker and more demoralizing than a prison cell. We can't imagine how dehumanizing it is.

I know just a bit about that because we've received thousands of letters from prisoners who read one of my books and wrote to say thank you. I read those letters, and the stories they tell about prison life are just unbelievable. You can watch all the prison movies you want, and when the movie is over, you can go to your kitchen and make a snack. You can get in your car and drive wherever you like. But those men and women are locked up, having lost their freedom for years, sometimes for life.

Prison is a disorienting experience. And it's no wonder John the Baptist temporarily lost his spiritual bearings and sent the messengers to Jesus with a question: "Are you the one who was to come, or should we expect someone else?" (Matt. 11:3 NIV). Now why do I bring up John the Baptist? Because when Jesus wanted to praise John the Baptist, he compared him to Elijah. "He is the Elijah who was to come" (Matt. 11:14 NIV). What Elijah was in the Old Testament, John the Baptist was in the New Testament. And both men struggled with depression and doubts. I believe that those whom God calls to do great, bold exploits are often the ones who are most prone to inner struggles with despondency and depression. In public John the Baptist is bold as a lion, yet put him in prison and he begins to lose his faith. Now here's Elijah, great man of God, spiraling downward, completely controlled by dark thoughts, filled with self-pity.

His Condition Diagnosed

If you study the biblical record, it seems clear that three things have happened to Elijah to bring him to this breaking point. These three things are understandable, they go together, and they can happen to any of us at any time.

First, he was overstrained mentally. It is possible to be under so much pressure for such a long period of time that the spring of life is wound so tightly and eventually it must break. Consider Elijah's career as a prophet. From the mountains of Gilead to the king's palace to the brook to the widow's home to the showdown on Mount Carmel, it's been one crisis after another. The late Tom Landry, coach of the Dallas Cowboys, was fond of saying, "Fatigue makes cowards of us all." Everyone has a limit. You've got your limit, and I've got mine. It's a good thing to realize when you've come to the end, and it's a good thing to realize before you get to the end.

You are not as smart as you think you are, and neither am I.

You are not as clever as you think you are, and neither am I.

You are not as resourceful as you think you are, and neither am I.

You are not as good under pressure as you think you are, and neither am I.

You are not as strong as you think you are, and neither am I.

You are not as wise as you think you are, and neither am I.

The mightiest oak tree in the forest can be easily brought down if you hit it with a tiny ax at just the right place. Elijah was overstrained mentally. He had pushed himself until he could push no longer.

Second, he was exhausted physically. At one point in his ministry, Jesus told his disciples to "come apart and rest for awhile" (see Mark 6:31). Vance Havner was fond of saying, "If we do not come apart and rest awhile, we will simply come apart." There is a time when you need to get up and go to work, and there is a time when you need to lie down and take a nap. Sometimes the best thing we can do for the Lord is to take a vacation. Play tennis. Ride your bike. Watch a football game. Knit a sweater. Have a date with your sweetheart. Play with your grandchildren. Eat an ice cream cone. Take an evening, make some popcorn, sit on the couch, and watch a video. There are times when God's work demands strenuous action. And there is a time when you need to sit in the recliner, crank it back, get a bowl of Cheetos and a Coke, pick up the remote control, and watch ESPN for a while. There is a time to be active and busy, and there is a time to relax. There is a time to write, a time to work, a time to preach, and a time to put on your helmet and go ride your bicycle. Solomon reminded us in Ecclesiastes 3 that there is a time for everything under the sun.

A time for war and a time for peace.
A time to sow and a time to reap.
A time to weep and a time to laugh.
A time to be born and a time to die.

"To everything there is a season." God ordains every season of life, including the times of hard work and the times when we must rest. In our twenty-first-century world, the reward tends to go to those who burn themselves out the quickest. Several years ago as I thought about the church I pastored for sixteen years, I made the following five observations about the congregation:

1. Down deep the people truly love the Lord. There is no question about that. If you got to know them personally, as I did for many years, you soon learned that their love for the Lord was genuine and heartfelt.

2. They are willing to serve the Lord. Like every church we always had a long list of vacancies in our various ministries, and every year we scrambled at the end of the summer to find enough teachers and helpers to begin the fall program. But every year, without fail, the Lord touched the hearts of our people, and they responded magnificently. I found that if you presented the right opportunity in the right way, the people were not unwilling to serve. Someone always stepped forward.

3. *Almost everyone in the church is overcommitted.* We all know about the 80/20 rule, which says that 20 percent of the people do 80 percent of the work and 80 percent of the people do 20 percent of the work. I'm sure there is some truth to that. And really, it's always true that an inner core of people in every congregation rise up and do the heavy lifting that must be done to move the Lord's work forward. But I'm not speaking about that at this point. I discovered that almost everyone at the church was overcommitted at home, on the job, in the neighborhood, in the community, in their families, in their extended families, in their church, and outside the church. Everyone is busy all the time.

4. *Almost everyone is overstressed.* This is the natural result of being busy and overcommitted. The demands of life create heavy burdens that wear you down after a while.

5. *People are easily distracted.* This is probably true of most churches, especially churches in metropolitan areas. People love the Lord, they are willing to serve, they are busy and thus overcommitted. One of the marks of an overstressed life is that you cannot keep your mind on anything for more than five minutes. People sometimes ask why I move around so much when I preach. One answer is that I keep moving to keep people's attention.

We live in an overcommitted, overstressed, overbusy generation where people are easily distracted. I discovered that it was easy for us to get the attention of people in the congregation, but it was almost impossible to hold that attention for very long. We would announce some great new initiative, and for fifteen minutes it's like the second coming of Pentecost, then fifteen minutes later people had forgotten what we had told them. That's a mark of an overstressed generation. If you live in a big city, that's just the way it is. And it's not that much different in small towns. We've got cable TV, high-speed Internet, instant messaging, video iPods, and satellite radio with one hundred channels so you can listen to your favorite station coast to coast. We live in an age of communications overload. Today when we teach young men how to preach, we tell them to be sure and change the subject every five minutes because that's the only way to hold people's attention. It wasn't that way fifty years ago. We communicate in bite-sized chunks because we are an easily distracted generation.

Third, Elijah was out of touch spiritually. "Elijah was afraid and ran for his life" (1 Kings 19:3 NIV). The Hebrew text contains a phrase that disappears in some modern translations. The first phrase of verse 3 literally reads, "And when he saw." That's his fundamental problem. His mind is overstressed. His body is physically exhausted. And now his eyes are off the Lord and they're on his circumstances. That's what happens when you are under enormous mental stress, when you are physically exhausted, when you've been running on Red Bull and four hours of sleep a night, and you've been burning the candle at both ends.

No wonder Elijah gets scared. He's been under enormous pressure for so long that he can't think clearly. Give him three nights of good sleep, and Jezebel won't bother him so much. When you have been under stress for a long time, you don't think clearly, and you make bad decisions that get you in trouble. That's why the little phrase in verse 3 is so important: "And when he saw." When he was on the mountain, all he could see was God. The prophets of Baal didn't bother him at all. The circumstances didn't matter. It was Elijah and God. But now in his state of emotional exhaustion, he sees Jezebel, he hears Jezebel, and where normally he would have stood his ground, he turns pale, runs for cover, keeps on running, and doesn't stop till he ends up in a cave on Mount Sinai hundreds of miles away.

So this is where we will leave the mighty prophet of God for the moment. He cowers in a cave, wishing to die, feeling utterly alone, lost in his own despair. But as we will see next time, God is not through with his servant yet. Though he ran as fast and as far as he could, Elijah could not outrun the Lord. God has much more work for him to do so Elijah can't stay in the cave forever. Though he made many mistakes, he is still God's man.

Stay tuned. God is about to turn Elijah's life around and use him again.

Chapter 9

OW TO HELP A CAVEMAN

"Fall seven times, stand up eight."
JAPANESE PROVERB

*W*e do live in strange times. Someone has called this the Age of Anxiety, and it seems appropriate enough. Not long ago I found this headline: "Most Think Country Headed in Wrong Direction." Those words could be slightly altered to read like this:

"Most Think Family Headed in Wrong Direction."
"Most Think Marriage Headed in Wrong Direction."
"Most Think Career Headed in Wrong Direction."
"Most Think World Headed in Wrong Direction."

Shortly before we moved from Chicago, we attended a worship service where the pastor said during a prayer, "It seems that we live in cataclysmic times," referring to recent earthquakes, hurricanes, and a tsunami in Asia that left hundreds of thousands dead and millions more impoverished. I thought later of the continuing unrest in North Korea, Iran, Iraq, across the Middle East, and threats of terrorism in Europe and America. A few days later I had lunch with a friend who is an executive working in Christian media. As we talked about recent terrorist threats, he commented that everyone in the restaurant was thinking, "When will it happen in Chicago?" While not everyone may have been thinking about it at precisely that instant, the fear that "it" will happen to us has been right beneath the surface ever since 9/11. I have often thought that the national blood pressure went up about one hundred points after 9/11 and has never really come down. Our fear makes us angry, uptight, tense, hostile, sullen, and impatient with one another. I see it on my bike rides because when you travel city streets, you live in constant awareness that drivers don't see you; if they see you, they don't notice you; and if they really do see you, they don't like you. So you constantly pay attention to the cars coming and going and often brushing right against you. I see the frustration on the faces of the drivers, and often I hear it when they honk their horns at the slightest provocation.

Lest you think I'm overstating it, the September 2005 issue of *Johns Hopkins Magazine* focused on the seven deadly sins: "Americans hate each other. There is not only the everyday empirical evidence of wrath along interstate highways, but in the snake pits of real estate, marriage, shopping, pro wrestling, and health insurance."[1]

So begins the article on "Anger" by Wayne Biddle. He adds this trenchant observation: "Anger seems nowadays just a millionth of an inch beneath every human surface, passive or aggressive, and it will bite your head off, stab you in the back, laugh in your face, leave you twisting in the wind—maybe all at once, and more."[2]

We do live in cataclysmic times, and the anger that lurks beneath the surface is a symptom of a world that seems to be spinning out of control. During lunch my friend and I spoke of the opportunities this provides for Christians to be bold about our faith. The Bible predicts a time in the last days when God will shake the nations so that those things that cannot be shaken will remain (Heb. 12:26–27). When Eugene Peterson paraphrased the last part of verse 27 in *The Message*, he said that God will shake the earth, "getting rid of all the historical and religious junk so that the unshakable essentials stand clear and uncluttered." Unshakable essentials. That says it all. God is shaking the earth so that we will figure out what matters most.

The Paths of Glory

In the end everything that man builds collapses before his eyes. A friend sent me an e-mail containing these lines from a poem by Thomas Gray (1716–71), "Elegy Written in a Country Churchyard" in England:

> *The boast of heraldry, the pomp of power*
> *And all that beauty, all that wealth e'er gave*
> *Awaits alike th' inevitable hour:*
> *The paths of glory lead but to the grave.*

According to 1 John 2:17, "The world is passing away along with its desires." Indeed, the best and brightest of us will someday die. All that we do will eventually be forgotten. Consider these next two sentences carefully:

Those who look to this world for approval will eventually be disappointed because the best things of this world must one day disappear.

Those who look to the God who created the world will find safety and security that will last forever.

What a revelation the judgment day will be for all of us. The things we thought were so important, so crucial, so vital, the things we included on our personal résumé, the degrees we earned, the money we made, the deals we closed, the classes we taught, the friends we cultivated in high places, the buildings we built, the organizations we managed, the budgets we balanced, the books we wrote, the songs we sang, the records we made, the trips we took, the portfolios we built, the fortunes we amassed, the positions we finally attained so that the people of the world and even our Christian friends would know that we didn't just sit on the couch watching *The Simpsons* every night, all that stuff we take such pride in, the things that in themselves are not evil or wrong or bad but are the "stuff" of life in this world, all of it, every single last bit of it, every part of it, considered singularly and then combined together to give us our reputation, our standing, our place in the world, even our place in the Christian world, our name in the lights, our claim to fame, our reason for existence, our bragging rights, if you will, the proof that we were here and made a name for ourselves in the short fifty or sixty or seventy or even eighty or ninety years that we have on planet Earth, think of it!, all of it added together means nothing, zip, zero, nada, vanity of vanities, all is vanity, and I think I've heard that somewhere before. That's a very long sentence, isn't it? I wrote it that way to emphasize how easy it is for us to get sucked into the world's way of thinking, how quickly it happens, and on so many different levels. All of it will someday amount to nothing.

If this sounds melancholy, I don't mean it that way. It's just the way the universe works. Nothing lasts forever, including you and me. We won't live forever on the earth. We are disposable, perishable creatures, "a flower quickly fading," here today and gone tomorrow. And we do live in cataclysmic times, in which God is shaking the world. That shaking will increase in the days to come as we near the return of Jesus Christ to the earth.

After living under the threat of terrorist attacks, rogue nuclear states, and being blindsided by earthquakes, tsunamis, and hurricanes, I don't blame anyone for feeling a bit shaky. Patience is in short supply everywhere. I ran across a little poem by Virginia Brasier that seems to describe contemporary life:

> This is the age of the half-read page
> And the quick bash, and the mad dash
> The bright night, with the nerves tight
> The plane hop, with a brief stop
> The lamp tan in a short span
> The big shot in a good spot
> And the brain strain and the heart pain
> And the cat-naps, till the spring snaps
> And the fun's done![3]

When last we met Elijah, he was in trouble. He was messed up, depressed, discouraged, stressed out, burned out, mentally fried, physically drained, and spiritually out of sorts. *He's exactly like many of us, in other words.* The third to the last line of that poem seems perfectly to describe him when it speaks of the brain strain and the heart pain. At some point, if you keep on pushing, the spring snaps and the fun's done. For Elijah the fun was done, at least for a while.

First Kings 19 not only tells us what happened to Elijah; it also describes how God met him at his lowest point. I happened to catch a few minutes of a leading Christian psychiatrist being interviewed on TV. After discussing the physical and medical factors that can lead to depression, he remarked that for most American Christians, depression is basically a spiritual issue. There is always a danger in a statement like that because people will read all sorts of things into it. Later he made clear that he believes in using all necessary medical means when that is appropriate to treat depression because there are often genuine medical issues involved. As I listened to him, I think he was trying to say that depression may be a symptom of underlying spiritual issues that need to be faced and addressed. Certainly Elijah was depressed and discouraged. After his great victory on Mount Carmel, I think he expected the nation to experience a vast turning to the Lord. But when Jezebel threatened him, he cracked under the pressure and ran south to Beersheba, and from Beersheba he went a day's journey into the desert. There he sat under a broom tree in utter dejection. Judging himself a failure, he prayed that God might take his life. F. W. Robertson pointed out that his predicament is common to all:

> What greater minds like Elijah's have felt intensely,
> all we have felt in our own degree. Not one of us but
> what has felt his heart aching for want of sympathy. We
> have had our lonely hours, our days of disappointment,
> and our moments of hopelessness, times when our high-
> est feelings have been misunderstood, and our purest
> met with ridicule. Days when our heavy secret was

lying unshared, like ice upon the heart. And then the spirit gives way: we have wished that all were over, that we could lie down tired, and rest like the children from life, that the hour was come when we could put down the extinguisher on the lamp, and feel the last grand rush of darkness on the spirit.[4]

Because we are all made of the same clay, let us pay close attention to how God deals with his discouraged servant. We find in the text that Elijah needed four things, and those four things he received from the Lord.

1. He needed rest and refreshment. Elijah sat under the broom tree so discouraged that he prayed that he might die. Then he fell asleep. The Lord sent an angel with a command from heaven: "All at once an angel touched him and said, 'Get up and eat'" (1 Kings 19:5 NIV). How's that for spiritual advice? Get up and eat. He doesn't say, "Get up and pray." He doesn't say, "Get up and read the Word." He doesn't say, "Get up and start preaching." He doesn't say, "Get up and serve the Lord." The angel tells Elijah to get something to eat.

Here's a profound truth. *Sometimes we need to eat.* Sometimes we need to sleep. Sometimes we need to eat and sleep even more than we need to pray. There's a time for everything. There is a time for crying out to God; and there is a time to roll over in bed, close your eyes, and get a good night's sleep. And there is a time when what you need is a Big Mac, French fries, and a chocolate milk shake. We all need a good night's sleep and a good meal. Sometimes we just need to let our hair down and have a blast. For some that means going waterskiing. For others it means hiking in the mountains. For some it means sitting in a comfortable chair and knitting with your friends. For me it means riding my bike.

That's why God commanded man to work for six days and to rest on the seventh day. God built into the fabric of the universe that we need to work and work hard and serve the Lord, and we also need some downtime. We need some rest, and we need some relaxation. Sometimes the most spiritual thing you can do is to get up and have a good meal because you'll feel so much better.

So the angel gave Elijah a specific command: "Get up and eat" (NIV). He looked around and found a cake of bread baked over hot coals and a jar of water. He ate and drank, and then he lay down and slept again. God's mountain man is tuckered out. He took a nap. He got up, had some food, and went back to bed again. Is he a sluggard? No. He's just worn out in the service of God. "The angel of the LORD came back a second time and touched him and said, 'Get up and eat, for the journey is too much for you'" (v. 7 NIV). Strengthened by that food, he traveled forty days and forty nights until he reached Horeb, the mountain of God. There he went into a cave and did what? He spent the night there.

Now understand, he's still got all kinds of problems. We've not gotten to the real issues of life yet. But sometimes you can't get to the deep issues until you deal with things like hunger and physical exhaustion. Basically God arranged for Elijah to have a six-week vacation, all expenses paid. That sounds good until you recall that he had to walk across the desert by himself to Mount Sinai.

Why did he go to Horeb? Because he knew Mount Sinai was the place you went when you know you need to meet God. He didn't pick just any mountain. If he wanted to find a cave, there were caves a lot closer than Horeb. He went back to where Moses met the Lord. There is a value in going back to certain places.

There's a value in going back to certain milestones in your life and certain physical locations in your life, places where you met God in the past.

When you are depressed, you need three things, and God made sure Elijah got all three of them.

You need good food.

You need some rest.

You need some physical exercise.

I would consider walking forty days across the desert good physical exercise. You need rest. You need food. You need exercise. You need more than that, but that's a good place to begin.

God's restoration of Elijah begins with rest and relaxation for the body, the mind, and the soul. But there is more to come.

2. He had to face his fears. "And the word of the LORD came to him. 'What are you doing here, Elijah?'" (v. 9 NIV). That's a good question. The last time we saw Elijah, he was winning a great victory on Mount Carmel. So what is he doing cowering in a cave, hundreds of miles away? Not that the Lord didn't know. This question was not for God's benefit but for Elijah's. "So explain yourself, son. You were my man up there on Mount Carmel. What are you doing here?" God was saying, "It's time to face your fears." This is Elijah's response: "I have been very zealous for the LORD God Almighty. The Israelites have rejected your covenant, broken down your altars, and put your prophets to death with the sword" (v. 10 NIV). Everything he said was true.

He had been zealous.

The people had rejected the covenant.

They put the prophets to death.

No exaggeration at all. If he had stopped there, he would have been on solid ground. Now look at the next sentence. "I am the only one left, and now they are trying to kill me too" (v. 10 NIV). The last part of that sentence is true; the first part was not true. But it was that first part, that feeling of being utterly alone, that needed an adjustment. He was so far gone in self-pity that he actually thought he was the only righteous man left in Israel.

Let me make a simple application. *Self-pity is the enemy of all spiritual growth.* As long as you feel sorry for yourself, you'll make a thousand excuses for not facing your own problems, and you'll never get better. A few years ago I met a man who got in trouble because of the Internet. He got drawn into pornography and ended up committing adultery. When the truth came out, it nearly cost him his marriage. He told me that part of the restoration process included going to a weekly meeting of men struggling with all sorts of sexual sins. It was a tough group. They had only one rule. No self-pity. No blaming your wife. No blaming your colleagues. No blaming your parents. No blaming your inner tendencies. No blaming something that happened to you when you were a child. If you started down that road, they would stop you. And he said, "If you continue with self-pity, they throw you out of the group because self-pity is the enemy of all spiritual growth. As long as you feel sorry for yourself, you cannot get better. As long as you blame others, you cannot get better." As long as you try to throw off your problems on somebody else, you cannot get better. And as long as you say, "I alone am left, O Lord, I am the only one who's faithful, I'm the only one on your team," as long as you talk like that, you cannot get better.

You may be stuck spiritually because you are wallowing in a sea of self-pity, and you have convinced yourself that your problems are caused by other people, and you make a career of blaming your circumstances and other people for your problems.

And you wonder why you aren't getting better. You are stuck, and you will be stuck until you stop making excuses and start taking responsibility. You cannot and you will not get better. *Self-pity is the mortal enemy of all spiritual growth.*

3. He needed a new vision of God. Note how these three things go together. Rest and relaxation speak to the body; facing his fears and his self-pity speaks to his mind; a new vision of God speaks to the need of his soul. He needed to be changed body, mind, and soul.

When Elijah began to wallow in self-pity, notice how God responded. Or more particularly notice what God *didn't* do. He didn't say what many of us would have said. "What is wrong with you? Get your act together." We would have argued with Elijah and told him to snap out of it. "Come on! Get a grip!" God didn't put Elijah down, rebuke him, or ridicule him. *Instead, God met him at the point of his deep despair.* He just said, "Son, come with me. Get up. That's right. Get up. Get out of your cave. Come on, Elijah. Come on out. I won't hurt you. Come on out of the cave. I want to show you something." That's all God did. He did not condemn him. As we know, condemning depressed people generally doesn't work. It doesn't help us when we're depressed if somebody condemns us, and it doesn't help for us to condemn somebody else. It just makes the situation worse.

What follows is amazing. A mighty wind tore across the face of the mountain, shattering the rocks. But the Lord was not in the wind. After the wind there was an earthquake. And after the earthquake there was a fire, but the Lord was not in the earthquake, and the Lord was not in the fire. And after the fire came a gentle whisper. When Elijah heard it, he pulled his cloak over his face, and he went out and stood in the mouth of the cave. F. W. Robertson has another helpful word at this point:

There are some spirits which must go through a discipline analogous to that sustained by Elijah. The storm-struggle must precede the still small voice. There are minds which must be convulsed with doubt before they can repose in faith. There are hearts which must be broken with disappointment before they can rise into hope. There are dispositions which, like Job, must have all things taken from them before they can find all things again in God. Blessed is the man who, when the tempest has spent its fury, recognizes his Father's voice in its under-tone, and bares his head and bows his knee, as Elijah did.[5]

Why does God put Elijah through this demonstration of divine power? *He's getting his man back in touch with spiritual reality.* Psalm 46:10 says, "Be still, and know that I am God." The Lord wants Elijah to know that it is not in the earthquakes or the fire or the huge events where we most often encounter the Lord. We more often meet God in the small, forgotten places of life. A few months ago I was complaining about something that had happened. My wife listened to me complain for a while, and then she listened some more. Finally she decided she had heard enough so she said what wives have said to complaining husbands since the beginning of time: "Grow up." I didn't like that at all. For one thing, I didn't want to grow up. I wanted to complain. So my wife said to me, "Stop complaining and open your eyes and see how good God has been to us." She was right, of course. We started to play a little game to see how many God sightings we could find every day. And do you know what we found? We discovered that if we paid attention, every day there were always a handful of God sightings, of God doing something—a phone call or somebody dropping by with an unexpected word of kindness or a card in the mail or an answered prayer. Sometimes it was just a little thing God would do, just something that caused us to say, "That was the Lord who did that for us." *We learned that if you keep your eyes open for God, pretty soon you'll see him everywhere.* Our problem is we want to see the earthquake; we want to see the fire all the time. We want the big demonstration. We want the spectacular answer to prayer. God says, "That's not always where you're going to see me, but just listen for the gentle whisper." *God always speaks loud enough for the willing ear to hear.* I have found myself praying over and over, "O Lord, open the eyes of my heart that I might see you everywhere." And you know what? It has enabled me to see God at work in places where I never saw him before.

During that same period I spent some time meditating on Psalm 42:5–6, "Why are you downcast, O my soul? Why so disturbed within me? Put your hope in God, for I will yet praise him, my Savior and my God" (NIV). The following thoughts came to mind:

1. The soul will sometimes be downcast and disturbed. This is part of the universal human experience.

2. Such times of disquiet (a word that seems appropriate in these days of noise and confusion and shouting voices) are not to be despised; much less are they to be denied. Part of our journey will include those times of inner turmoil and soul disturbance.

3. We should not deny the truth about our own condition. This week I read a funeral sermon for a pastor who committed suicide. The man giving the sermon (a former seminary classmate) used as his text the words of Jesus in

Matthew 5:3, "Blessed are the poor in spirit, for theirs is the kingdom of heaven." We are all poor in spirit, he said, and part of our poverty lies in the fact that we don't realize how broken we are. Often it takes a tragedy to show us the truth. How desperately we all need the grace of God. How hopeless we are without it.

4. The psalmist felt overwhelmed by his enemies who were oppressing him (Ps. 42:1–2). He felt that God himself had abandoned him ("Why have you rejected me?"). Our enemies will almost always be the folks closest to us. We are told to love our neighbors and to love our enemies because they are often the same people. And that sort of pressure can drain the life right out of your soul.

5. What do you do when you can't change your outward circumstances? Your only hope lies in changing your inner circumstances. The psalmist practiced a little godly self-talk. He talked to his own soul. For many people self-talk only makes things worse, but here it makes things better. He asks his soul, "Why are you downcast?" Good question. Perhaps we should all look in the mirror and ask, "What's wrong with you?" The answer may surprise us.

6. He gave his soul an order: "Put your hope in God."

7. He added a promise: "I will yet praise him."

8. He tied it to God's promise and his faithfulness: "My Savior and my God."

Spurgeon has a nice thought about the little word "yet." "Oh! what a glorious 'yet' that is. How it swims! Never was there a swimming suit like that which is made of hope."[6]

When these moments come, and they come to all of us again and again, we must do what the psalmist did. Talk to your soul.

Find out why your soul is upset. Tell your soul to trust in the Lord. And make a determination that when the trial is over and the dark clouds lift, you will "yet" praise his name. Finally, to borrow another phrase from Spurgeon, "follow hard after God." If you focus on your troubles, you will sink ever deeper. If you focus on the Lord, at least you have set your compass in the right direction. You may still be in the darkness, but if you follow hard after God, the light will shine again.

Trust in the Lord thy God always,
and thou the time shalt see,
To give him thanks with laud and praise,
for health restored to thee.
—*The Scottish Psalter, 1635*

4. He needed a new commission. In verse 13 God repeats his question, and Elijah repeats his answer. There are times when a mistake must be corrected with accurate information. So now God is going to give Elijah some accurate information. The Lord said to him, "Go back the way you came, and go to the Desert of Damascus" (v. 15 NIV). That's a long journey from the Sinai desert, through the Holy Land, all the way up to the desert around Damascus. Then he has some specific instructions: "When you get there, anoint Hazael king over Aram. Also, anoint Jehu son of Nimshi king over Israel, and anoint Elisha son of Shaphat from Abel Meholah to succeed you as prophet. Jehu will put to death any who escape the sword of Hazael, and Elisha will put to death any who escape the sword of Jehu. Yet I reserve seven thousand in Israel—all whose knees have not bowed down to Baal and all whose mouths have not kissed him" (vv. 15–18 NIV).

God reminds Elijah that he's not alone. Not only is God with him; God has another seven thousand in Israel who have not bowed down to Baal. Understand there is no spot in this world so lonely where God is not already there. God is not just to be seen in the big things of life. He's also to be seen in the stillness and in the small things. God is not limited by your small vision. In all of this God is reminding Elijah, "You are not alone; I am with you and I've got seven thousand more just like you. I'm going to give you a man to be your protégée, your partner, and your successor. You never were alone, you're not alone now, and you're not going to be alone in the future." Elijah had accomplished more than he thought. Those seven thousand were men and women who took strength from Elijah's brave confrontation with the prophets of Baal. So his life had not been wasted after all. *No life is wasted that is spent in the service of our Lord who promised to reward even a cup of cold water given in his name.* And this is the ultimate irony of the story. Elijah thought he had failed, but out of his perceived failure came assurance of his ultimate victory in the lives he touched who, like him, would not bow down to Baal.

Learn this lesson. *You are not in a position to estimate your own effectiveness.* When you think you have won, don't be so sure. When you think you have failed, let God render the final verdict. You and I are as likely as Elijah to estimate wrongly both our victories and our defeats. Better to do our best and leave the results with God. He knows better than we do the lives that have been changed by our service for Christ.

If Satan cannot get to us externally, he'll get to us internally. *It is no surprise that Elijah's greatest victory and his greatest defeat come back to back.* It is not a sin to be discouraged. It is not a sin to be depressed. It's what you do when you are discouraged, depressed, and feeling hopeless that matters. Don't fight the battle alone. Get some help. Get all the help you need. And remember this: God is still there. There's no pit so deep that the love of God is not deeper still. If you are discouraged, be encouraged. The Lord still loves you. You are not alone because the Lord has not forgotten you.

Keep believing.

Never give up.

The Lord is on your side.

Chapter 10

BURNING THE PLOW

"The call of God embarrasses us because of two things—it presents us with sealed orders and urges us to a vast venture."
OSWALD CHAMBERS

Elijah was not the most balanced man in the Bible. If you made a list of adjectives that described him, *balanced* would probably not make the top fifty. It's hard to call a rough-hewn mountain man balanced. What do you say about a man who . . .

Faced down a wicked king.

Lived by a brook where he was fed by ravens.

Lived with a widow.

Raised a dead boy to life.

Challenged the king again.

Called for a public confrontation.

Ridiculed other religions.

Mocked the prophets of Baal.

Called down fire from heaven.
Slaughtered the prophets of Baal.
Outran the king's chariot.
Ran from the queen.
Prayed that he might die.
Hiked forty days across the desert.
Hid in a cave.
Heard God's voice.
Claimed to be the only righteous man left.

What do you say about a man like that? Say what you want, but don't call him balanced.

Balance is in vogue today. *We all want to be balanced so that all the areas of life are in harmony.* When we choose leaders, we look for people with balanced temperaments, who can balance the demands of home and work, who react to a crisis with a balanced approach, who know how to balance competing demands and find a workable compromise.

Balance is good. Balance is cool. Balance is overrated.

There aren't a lot of balanced men in the Bible. Not Moses. He was a hothead who killed an Egyptian and then tried to cover it up. David? Not by a long shot. Jacob? Are you kidding? Daniel? Not after that episode with the handwriting on the wall. Paul wasn't such an easy man to work with. Just ask Barnabas. And Peter? He's the man with the foot-shaped mouth. He was brave until a teenaged girl challenged him. Then the bold apostle crumbled.

Elijah was *not* balanced. He was headstrong, determined, impetuous, prone to emotional excess; and he was a deeply devoted follower of God.

He was God's man. God's prophet. God's spokesman to an evil and unbelieving generation. Balance is good, but sometimes you need a man who seems about "a half bubble off center." Regular types need not apply. Elijah fit the bill perfectly.

Now God is about to give Elijah a protégé, an apprentice, a young man whom he could mentor. God knew that Elijah needed a friend who could walk with him and share his burdens. He needed someone who could continue the work after he was gone.

Enter Elisha. When first we meet him, he is plowing a field. But soon he will burn his plow, say farewell to his family, and give up his security to follow this wild mountain man wherever God leads him.

First there was Elijah.

Now there is Elisha.

Behind them both stands God.

Let us see what lessons we can glean from the calling of Elisha.

God's call forces us to make difficult choices. "So Elijah went from there and found Elisha son of Shaphat. He was plowing with twelve yoke of oxen, and he himself was driving the twelfth pair. Elijah went up to him and threw his cloak around him" (1 Kings 19:19 NIV).

It is not without significance that Elisha was plowing in the fields when Elijah threw his cloak around him. To us that simple act would have passed without meaning, but Elisha knew exactly what Elijah meant. *A prophet's cloak was a distinctive garment, such as John the Baptist's cloak of camel's hair (Matt. 3:4).* Placing a prophetic cloak on Elisha was like a king giving his scepter to his son. It was a sign of divine calling.[1]

And where does Elijah find his man? In the field with twelve yoke of oxen (the sign of a wealthy family), with Elisha himself driving the twelfth pair. It wasn't as if he were looking for a new job. Elisha had his hands full running the family farm. Ask anyone who grew up on a farm, and they will tell you the work never ends. Tending the animals, keeping the fields in shape, preparing to plant and harvest, dealing with the changing weather and the problems of your workers, juggling a thousand details every day—to keep on top of everything and do it all the time, you have to get up early and stay up late. Lazy men need not apply for the job. If you are a farmer, you live your work all day every day. I doubt that Elisha had any thought that before sundown he would slaughter his oxen and burn his plow. I'm sure that was nowhere on his radar screen when the day began.

But this is how God often works. He calls us when we are in the midst of our daily routine. He called Moses while he was tending Jethro's flocks. He called David while he was tending his father's sheep. He called Nehemiah, who had a hugely important job as cupbearer to the king. He called Peter when he was a fisherman and Matthew when he was a tax collector. He called Elisha when he was plowing the field. We are far more likely to encounter God by getting out of bed and getting busy doing our job than if we stay in bed waiting for a dream or a vision.

That leads to a profound insight: *99 percent of life is ordinary.* It's just the same old stuff day after day. You get up in the morning, take a shower, put on your clothes, eat breakfast, get the kids ready for school, go to work, hope the kids are OK, come back from work dead tired, read the paper, watch TV, try to be nice, eat supper, play with the kids, flop into bed dead tired, get up the next morning, and then do it all over again. That's the way life is. It's the same old thing day after day. Where do you begin in discovering the will of God? *You begin by doing what you already know to be the will of God in your present situation.* So many of us live for those high mountain-peak experiences, for those times when the clouds part and God seems so close to us.

Get up and do it! Many people wish those spectacular moments would happen every day. Often when we say, "God, show me your will," what we really mean is, "Lord, give me some feeling, some insight, some spiritual revelation." And God says, "I have already shown you my will. Now just get up and do it!"

- What is God's will for a student? God's will for a student is to do his/her homework.
- What is God's will for a doctor? Get up and do your rounds early in the morning.
- What is God's will for a pharmacist? Take extra care as you fill those prescriptions.
- What is God's will for a banker? Take care of the money entrusted to you.
- What is God's will for an accountant? Take care of those books, and do it right.
- What is God's will for a teacher? Do your lesson plans and come to class ready to teach.
- What is God's will for a salesman? Know your product, make your contacts, and move the merchandise.
- What is God's will for a football coach? Get your team ready to play the big game on Friday night.
- What is God's will for an assembly-line worker? Show up on time, sober, with a good attitude, ready to work.
- What is God's will for a flight attendant? Be on time, be in uniform with a smile on your face.

If you are a young mother and want to know what God's will is, it has something to do with dirty diapers. God's will for young mothers is *more* than dirty diapers, but it's not *less* than that. God's will for a secretary is *more* than typing, but it's not *less* than that. God's will for you is more than showing up and doing a job. But it is not less than that.

So many of us want to live only on the mountaintop. That's not where you discover God's will. *You discover God's will in the nitty-gritty of the valley every single day.* The Bible says, "Whatever your hand finds to do, do it with all your might" (Eccles. 9:10). Why should God show you his will for the future if you aren't doing the will of God in the present?

Everything changed when Elijah showed up. No one had to tell Elisha who he was. Everyone knew his name and his face. People couldn't stop talking about how he called down fire from heaven and defeated the prophets of Baal. The whole nation knew about this strange, enigmatic, rough-hewn mountain man from Gilead who seemed to fear no one. He also seemed to appear and disappear without warning. No one knew where he was or what he was doing, and then bam! There he was again. Suddenly he showed up at Elisha's family farm, three hundred miles from the cave on Mount Horeb.

It seems to have happened this way. Without a word Elijah strides up to Elisha, takes off his cloak, and puts it on Elisha. And then he begins to walk away. Elisha knew what it meant. Elijah was offering him a job. Now the young man had a choice to make. *He could stay with the oxen, or he could follow the prophet's call.* The life of a farmer was hard, but for Elisha it was also safe. He could stay with the oxen and keep plowing furrows, one after another, or he could walk away from all of it, into an unknown future which, if you consider the recent events on Mount Carmel, might get him into some hot water.

God has placed inside every man a desire to find an adventure to live. That's why men love fast cars, football, and movies like *Braveheart* and *The Dirty Dozen*. It's also why we don't watch *Sleepless in Seattle* unless there's a woman involved. Men were born for adventure, we were hardwired by God to take risks; we were made to glance at our cards, look around the table, take a deep breath, and say, "All in." I'm not saying women don't do that because they do, but it's different because men and women are different. Elisha chose the hard path of risk instead of playing it safe. It's not like Elijah gave him a job description with fancy perks. Years ago I remember seeing a sign advertising for young people to join the California Conservation Corps. The sign read "Long Hours, Hard Work, Low Pay." That's pretty much the job description for a prophet. Elisha knew that going in, and he didn't hesitate.

God's call leads to painful separation. "Elisha then left his oxen and ran after Elijah. 'Let me kiss my father and mother good-by,' he said, 'and then I will come with you.' 'Go back,' Elijah replied. 'What have I done to you?'" (v. 20 NIV). We learn several useful things from Elisha's response.

First, it is an immediate response. He left his oxen and ran after Elijah. Why did he run? Because Elijah wasn't staying around to discuss the matter. He placed his cloak on Elisha and then started walking away. Elisha ran because if he didn't, Elijah would soon have disappeared.

Second, it is a humble response. While he accepts the call, he asks Elijah for permission to say farewell to his parents.

Third, it is a human response. He does not wish to disappear suddenly and leave his parents to wonder where he went and why. Elisha appears to have been a family man in the best sense of that word. Though God's call will now lead him into a new arena of activity, that departure is not to be accomplished without taking time to say farewell.

The purpose here is clear. Elisha is not going back to ask his parents for permission. He is old enough to respond on his own. But because he is a faithful son, he will not leave them in the lurch. Some may recall the case of the would-be disciple who upon being called by Christ, asked for permission to go back and bury his father (Luke 9:59). But in that case, the man meant, "Let me go home and stay with my father until he dies. When he is gone, then I will follow you." *But such a reason is little more than an excuse cloaked in filial piety.* The man never wanted to follow Jesus. Taking care of his father was just a pious excuse. Elisha is not like that at all. He wishes to say farewell to his family (as he should), and then he will gladly follow Elijah.

Here we come face-to-face with the high cost of following Jesus. I met a couple whose son serves Christ in a distant land. He is so far away from America that it took nine separate plane flights to reach a certain remote town in the jungle on the other side of the world. Once the couple got to that remote town, they had to take overland transportation to reach their son and his wife. They have gone to the literal "ends of the earth" to bring the gospel to a tribe that knows nothing about Jesus. They have devoted themselves to learning the language, reducing it to writing, translating the New Testament, and someday learning to preach the good news in that language. They are doing this for the sake of five hundred tribal people somewhere in the jungle on the far side of the earth. As we talked with the parents, we could sense the solemn joy mixed with sorrow at having their son and his wife so far away, living in the most primitive conditions.

But this has always been part of the high cost of the Great Commission. *Following Jesus always leads to a cross where our dreams are crucified.* If you follow him, you may end up in Tampa or Sacramento or Boston or Singapore. Who knows? You might end up in a ranch house in suburbia or a crowded apartment in Beijing. You might even get married and head for the jungle. But there is a cross, always a cross, for the followers of Jesus. If we take the words of our Lord seriously, our sons and daughters may end up doing things that shock us and even anger us. Jesus said as much in Luke 14:26. "If anyone comes to me and does not hate his father and mother, his wife and children, his brothers and sisters—yes, even his own life—he cannot be my disciple" (NIV). Jesus does not mean that following him will cause us to hate our parents. Far from it. Following Jesus ought to strengthen our love for our family. But it does mean that following Jesus has a price tag attached to it that we dare not disregard. *Faithfulness to Christ may lead us to do things that those closest to us will not understand or support.* They may think that we hate them when all we are doing is following Christ.

The parents I mentioned miss their son and daughter-in-law terribly and rarely get to see them. But they offered their son to the Lord when he was born, and they have never gone back on that commitment. So there are sorrow and joy and solemn pride in their voices when they speak of him. And as I read the e-mail updates he and his wife send back from the jungle, I sense joy and determination and even exhilaration as he and his young bride day after day live with tribal people who never bathe because of their fear of evil spirits. They long for the day when they can speak the good news in words "their tribe" can understand. That day is still several years away, but it comes closer all the time. If you asked them, "Is the sacrifice worth it?" they would say they haven't sacrificed anything. They are only following God's call. Someone has said that for the Christian, sacrifice is "the ecstasy of giving the best you have to the one you love the most." As they make their home in the jungle on the other side of the world, the young couple would agree with that statement.

Several years ago I spent a week ministering to a group of retired missionaries in Sebring, Florida. I suppose that the average age of the missionaries was seventy-five to eighty and their accumulated years of service must total several thousand years. I met aged saints of God who went to Africa in the 1930s and 40s, many of them serving for decades sharing Christ in difficult Muslim territory. Nearly all of them served forty years on the field; some of them stayed sixty years before returning to America. It was humbling to be around such fine, cheerful, godly saints whose hearts still respond to the call of the Great Commission. They shared stories of things that happened in Africa forty-five to fifty years ago as if they had happened yesterday. They have all known the sorrows of life full well, but there is a joy among them and a peace and a sense of trust in God that outweigh any difficulties they have faced. And since they are elderly, they all face health problems and the knowledge that life is short. So their joy is all the more remarkable and uplifting. And I noticed something else besides their joy.

No regrets.

The missionaries all knew their share of hardship, discouragement, opposition, sickness, frustration, loneliness, physical suffering, and spiritual warfare. But they do not dwell on these matters. They seem to have "counted it all joy" for the sake of serving Christ. And each morning they eagerly pray that God might grant further victories for the gospel around the world. Any of them could have had an easier life in the United States, but they heard the call of God, and that settled the matter for them. Some of them endured many years of difficulties, and those who labored in Muslim lands often saw only a handful of converts at the end of it all. I heard one of them quote an early missionary who said, "Focus on the cross and not on the hardness of the Muslim religion." That is what they have done; and they built hospitals, clinics, schools, churches, and mission stations in remote areas. Now they are seventy-five, eighty, eighty-five, ninety years old and living their final years. Instead of regret, they have visible joy and deep satisfaction with how things have turned out. It is bracing and good for the soul to be around saints of God who have no regrets and gladness of heart. The world barely knows they are here. In heaven their names are written in gold.

We used to sing a song called "Joy in Serving Jesus." The first line, "There is joy in serving Jesus," came to my mind as I thought about my friends and their son and daughter-in-law deep in the jungle and again as I thought about the retired missionaries in Florida. Following Christ always leads to painful separation from the things of the world and sometimes even from our own flesh and blood, but there is joy in recompense that outweighs the cost.

Elisha would miss his family, and they would miss him. Nothing would ever be the same again. Never again would Elisha stand behind oxen while they plowed the field. To paraphrase Jesus, now Elisha would be plowing for men.

God's call requires decisive action. "So Elisha left him and went back. He took his yoke of oxen and slaughtered them. He burned the plowing equipment to cook the meat and gave it to the people, and they ate. Then he set out to follow Elijah and became his attendant" (v. 21 NIV). You can't sit on the fence forever. Elisha had a few seconds to make a life-changing decision. Once he signed on to be Elijah's apprentice, he had to burn his bridges so that when things got tough, he wouldn't be tempted to go back to his old life.

That's why he slaughtered his oxen.

That's why he burned his plow.

And he didn't do it in secret either. He threw himself a going-away party and invited everyone he knew. He cooked the meat from the oxen and then gave it to the people. It was his way of saying, "The old life is gone forever. A new day has come for me." Just as I typed those words, I thought of Billy Sunday, the famous baseball player turned evangelist. His story has a special place in my heart because for almost a decade, I played the part of Billy Sunday and reenacted his life at his grave site in Forest Home Cemetery in Forest Park, Illinois. It was part of the annual "Tale of Tombstones" sponsored by the local historical society. I told the story of Billy Sunday's colorful life and his conversion in 1886 at the Pacific Garden Mission. As Billy himself told the story, he was standing outside a saloon with some of his teammates from the Chicago White Stockings (today called the Chicago Cubs) when a "gospel wagon" from the mission came down the street. Gripped with conviction of sin, he turned to his friends and said, "Boys, I've come to the end of the line. I'm through with the old life, and I'm heading in a new direction." That marked the turning point of his life. A few nights later after hearing Harry Monroe preach at the mission, he gave his heart to Christ. For the rest of his life, including his amazing evangelistic career in which he preached in person to one hundred million people, he never tired of referring to the day he made a decision to follow Jesus.

When God calls, you have to make a decision. The burning of the plow takes on deep significance in light of Jesus' words in Luke 9:62, "No one who puts his hand to the plow and looks back is fit for service in the kingdom of God" (NIV).

It's not wrong to plow a field, but if your plowing keeps you from Jesus, you'd better burn the plow.

Anything good can become a hindrance if it keeps you from following the Lord.

Elisha was saying, "I'm following God's call, and no matter what happens, I'm not going back. The old life is over forever. A new day has come for me."

The hard is what makes it good. Not long ago I watched (for the fifth or sixth time) *A League of Their Own*, starring Tom Hanks and Geena Davis. Near the end of the film, the team coached by Tom Hanks is about to play in the All-American Girls' Baseball World Series during World War II. Geena Davis, the star catcher, has decided to go home because her husband has returned from the war. Hanks confronts her by reminding her of how much she loves the game.

"I don't love it," she says, "not like you."

"Oh yes you do," Hanks replies. "It's in your blood."

"I can't do it," she says. "It's too hard."

At that moment Tom Hanks turns slightly, grabs his face, grimaces, and then says, "You're right. It is hard. It's supposed to be hard. The hard is what makes it good." With that he joins the rest of the team on the bus while Geena Davis leaves with her husband. Later she returns in time for the seventh and deciding game of the series.

"It's supposed to be hard. The hard is what makes it good."

That's not just true about baseball. That's the truth about the Christian life.

It is hard.

It's supposed to be hard.

The hard is what makes it good.

If it were easy, anyone could do it. But not everyone can. Not everyone can walk the Christ road.

The hard is what makes it good.

If your name is Elisha and a mountain man throws his cloak on your back, you'd better follow him. But before you go, make sure you burn the plow so you can't go back when the going gets rough.

And it will get rough. It always does.

There will be hard days, bad days, sad days, discouraging days, confusing days, angry days, frustrating days, boring days, upsetting days, discombobulating days, and then there will be some really bad days.

The hard is what makes it good.

Martin Luther had something to say about this in the hymn "A Mighty Fortress Is Our God":

> Let goods and kindred go, this mortal life also.
> The body they may kill. God's truth abideth still.
> His kingdom is forever.

Stop your complaining. Stop your bellyaching. Stop your moaning. Stop dreaming of happier times and an easier road.

The hard is what makes it good.

And the good is better than you've ever dreamed. It's out of this world.

Pick up your cross and follow him. It's not easy, but it's not supposed to be easy.

Pick it up anyway. Follow him. Go where he leads. It's the one decision you'll never regret.

Chapter 11

PAYDAY SOMEDAY

"The arm of the universe is long, but it bends toward justice."
MARTIN LUTHER KING JR.

Three years have passed since the showdown on Mount Carmel. During those three years the people of Israel defeated the vastly superior Syrian army, which resulted in a period of peace and prosperity. And it is fair to say that along with that peace and prosperity, Baal worship apparently had taken its previous high place in the people's affections. Despite the slaughter of the prophets of Baal on top of Mount Carmel, it was still true that Ahab was the king; it was still true that wicked Jezebel was his wife. And as long as Ahab was the king and Jezebel was his wife, Baal worship would still grip the nation. But we have moved now three years down the road.

Ahab has his summer palace in a place called Jezreel. He has come to that palace for a few days of rest. One day Ahab is out walking, looking, and thinking. There next to the summer palace of Jezreel, nestled right up against it, is the vineyard of a man by the name of Naboth.[1]

The Main Characters of the Story

The story I'm going to tell you has four main characters. *I introduce to you first Naboth, a good and godly man, a man who worshipped the Lord and followed the law of his God.* He was one of the seven thousand who had not bowed the knee to Baal. It happened that he owned a vineyard next to the summer palace of wicked king Ahab. We may assume that up until this day there had never been any trouble between Naboth and Ahab. So far as we know, Ahab had paid no attention to Naboth, and Naboth had done whatever he needed to do to stay out of the way of the wicked king. But one day Ahab saw Naboth's vineyard and decided he wanted it. That covetous lust would set in motion a disastrous chain of events.

The second key player is Ahab. About him we need only say what we have already said, that no more wicked king ever sat upon the throne of Israel. Holy Scripture declares that he more than any other man imported the worship of Baal into Israel. For that and that alone there is a black mark forever, always, and eternally over his name. He is the king, though I think it would be fair to say his life and his mind are really controlled by the third character in this story.

Her name is Jezebel. If Ahab was a wicked toad squatting on the throne of Israel, then Jezebel was an evil snake coiled around the throne. She was not Jewish. She was a pagan woman out and out. She came from a long line of Baal worshippers in the

Sidonian region of south Lebanon. When she married Ahab, she brought her wicked religion into Israel with her. And I suppose we should say this. Between Ahab and Jezebel, if you had to say who was worse, you would say that he was weak and she was strong. Ahab was easily influenced, and she was always ready to push her husband in the wrong direction.

So far we've got Naboth who owns the vineyard, a godly man, a common man, a workingman, a man who appears here and here only on the pages of the Bible. Then we have Ahab the king and Jezebel his wife.

And fourth, as we shall see eventually as the story unfolds, we have God's mountain man, Elijah the Tishbite. Since his great victory on Mount Carmel and his humiliating running away and going down to the cave in Mount Horeb, Elijah has not been heard from for three years. To be truthful, we really don't know what he's been doing for those three years. But as far as we can tell, the man of God made his last public appearance on top of Mount Carmel. Soon he will return to the public stage.

The Unfolding of the Story

But the story begins on that day in Jezreel when Ahab looked at the vineyard of Naboth and said to himself, "I'm the king of Israel. I need this vineyard, and I want this vineyard for myself." So Ahab went to Naboth and said, "Would you please sell your vineyard to me? If you will not sell your vineyard to me, would you please trade it? I am the king. If you will give me your vineyard, I will give you another piece of land here in Israel that is worth much more." I pause here to say the king was within his rights to do this. He had every right to go to Naboth. He did not sin by making that sort of offer. It was a perfectly legitimate thing for him to do. However, he didn't count on the fact that Naboth was a man of God who followed the law of God. Here is his simple reply to the king: "The LORD forbid that I should give you the inheritance of my fathers" (1 Kings 21:3). One simple sentence. Those are the only recorded words of Naboth, but they tell us all we need to know.

1. He was a man who respected the Lord.
2. He was a man who respected the Lord's word.
3. He was a man who respected his own spiritual heritage.

He refused to sell the vineyard because Numbers 36:7 said that if a family had been given a plot of land, it was to be handed down from father to son from generation unto generation. It was not to be sold. It was to be in the hands of the family forever. That was God's command. So Naboth said to the king, "The Lord forbid that I should do anything that should sully my family's inheritance and break the law of my God." In other words, "No deal, O King. I am sorry but I cannot do business with you today."

Naturally the king was upset, humiliated, and angry. He went back to his palace in a big funk. "So Ahab went home, sullen and angry because Naboth the Jezreelite had said, 'I will not give you the inheritance of my fathers.' He lay on his bed sulking and refused to eat" (v. 4 NIV). The king threw a fit. When the queen asked why he was so grouchy, he replied, "Because I said to Naboth the Jezreelite, 'Sell me your vineyard; or if you prefer, I will give you another vineyard in its place.' But he said, 'I will not give you my vineyard'" (v. 6 NIV). He neglected to tell his wife the real reason—that Naboth would not sell because he would not violate the law of God.

Jezebel had a plan. "Is this how you act as king over Israel? Get up and eat! Cheer up. I'll get you the vineyard of Naboth the Jezreelite" (v. 7 NIV). So wicked Jezebel hatched a diabolical plot. She decided to write a letter in the name of the king. She forged his name, although I suppose you can't really call it forgery because he acquiesced in what she did. She composed the letter and had it sent to the elders of the town. The text of the letter she wrote is actually in the Bible. "Proclaim a day of fasting and seat Naboth in a prominent place among the people. But seat two scoundrels opposite him and have them testify that he has cursed both God and the king. Then take him out and stone him to death" (vv. 9–10 NIV). We call this a kangaroo court, a setup from the get-go. "So the elders and nobles who lived in Naboth's city did as Jezebel directed" (v. 11 NIV). The whole city had become so corrupt that the so-called spiritual leaders, instead of protesting this evil murderous plot, went along with Jezebel's plan.

But it gets worse in verse 12: "They proclaimed a fast." Can you imagine that? A fast which was to be unto the Lord. "They proclaimed a fast and seated Naboth in a prominent place among the people" (NIV). That doesn't mean they're about to give him a prize. That means he's about to be sentenced. "Then two scoundrels came and . . . brought charges against Naboth . . . , saying, 'Naboth has cursed both God and the king'" (v. 13 NIV). Complete lies. "So they took him outside the city and stoned him to death" (v. 13 NIV).

Jezebel sent word to the king that the vineyard was now his. We find out later in 2 Kings 9 that they also killed his two sons, thus leaving no living heirs, which meant the land now reverted to the crown. When Ahab saw that the land was his, he was pleased.

"Arise, Elijah"

It appears that the king and his wife have gotten away with murder. Read the story. You say, "Where is God? Does he not know? Does he not care? Where is God when one of his own is put to death? Where is God when a man of God is killed for doing right? Where is God when the wicked rise to power? Where is God when a man like Ahab and a woman like Jezebel can get away with murder? Where is God when evil is let loose in the world?"

But that is not the end of the story. Recall the words of Proverbs 15:3, "The eyes of the LORD are everywhere, keeping watch on the wicked and the good" (NIV). God had been watching the whole scene from heaven. Now he was about to act.

God came to his prophet, patted him on the shoulder, and told him to head for Jezreel. In the King James Version Jezebel told Ahab to "arise" and take the vineyard, and God said the same thing to Elijah. "Arise, prophet of God, I have a job for you to do." Three long years had passed since the last time the prophet had spoken publicly. I don't know if Elijah had wondered if God had put him on the shelf. Perhaps Elijah feared that his running away had caused God to give up on him. Maybe he thought his days of prophesying were over. *But God knew all along he had another job for his man. He was just waiting for the right time.* When Jezebel said, "Arise," God said to Elijah, "Arise, go find that wicked king. Deliver a message from me."

"Go down to meet Ahab king of Israel, who rules in Samaria. He is now in Naboth's vineyard, where he has gone to take possession of it. Say to him, 'This is what the LORD says: Have you not murdered a man and seized his property?' Then say to him, 'This is what the LORD says: In the place where dogs licked up Naboth's blood, dogs will lick up your blood—yes, yours!'" (vv. 18–19 NIV).

When Elijah delivers his message, he adds an interesting phrase in verse 20: "I have found you, . . . because you have sold yourself to do evil in the eyes of the LORD" (NIV). The Hebrew word translated "sold yourself" has a secondary meaning, "to marry." Elijah says to Ahab, "You have married evil, and in marrying evil you have given yourself completely to it." There will be disaster in Ahab's family, his dynasty will come to an end, and dogs will consume Jezebel. The dogs will feed on those who die in the city, and the birds will eat the flesh of those who die in the country.

Elijah delivered the message, and then he disappeared. This seems to be a pattern with him. He just shows up, delivers his message, and then bam! He's gone.

Ahab Gets the Point

Days turned into weeks. Weeks turned into months. Ahab didn't hear from Elijah again. Every time he heard a dog bark, he jumped. I think he never got it out of his mind. One day Ahab decided he wanted to go to war against Ben-Hadad, the king of Syria, the man he had defeated earlier whom he should have killed when he had the chance, but he didn't. Now he was going to go to war against him a second time, only this time it was not going to work out so well. He asked Jehoshaphat, the king of Judah, to join him in his war against Ben-Hadad. Jehoshaphat agreed, and the day came when they were ready to go to battle. Knowing that he was a marked man, Ahab told Jehoshaphat to go to battle dressed as a king and he (Ahab) would go out dressed as a common soldier. What Ahab didn't know was that Ben-Hadad had given an unusual order to his army. He told his army to concentrate only on killing Ahab. When the battle started, the Syrians spotted

Jehoshaphat and were about to kill him, thinking he was Ahab. Suddenly someone shouted, "We've got the wrong king." In the confusion of battle, one of the Syrian archers shot an arrow at random. He wasn't aiming at anything. He saw the army of Israel and shot an arrow toward them. Ahab was dressed in armor like a regular soldier. The arrow just "happened" to come down and hit Ahab. The Bible says it hit between the sections of his armor. You could never do that on purpose. It's not even a million-to-one shot. That would be way too low. The soldier shot the arrow, and in the sovereign hand of God it went up, came down, and hit Ahab in the chink of his armor. He began to bleed profusely until the blood covered the floor of his chariot. But he would not leave the battlefield. When he died that evening, the army began to scatter. They buried Ahab in Samaria.

Now they had a chariot covered with his blood. They took it to the Ajax Chariot Wash and washed out the chariot. We're told it was where the prostitutes went to do their bathing. When they washed out the blood, there was so much of it that the dogs came and licked it up, just as Elijah had said.

Jezebel Goes to the Dogs

Shortly after this Elijah was taken to heaven in a fiery chariot. He's gone. He's off the scene. He's in heaven with the Lord. Five years pass. Ten years pass. Elijah's long gone. He's been replaced by Elisha. Jezebel is an older woman now. She is still *the* power in the nation of Israel. It seems as if Elijah was right about Ahab and wrong about Jezebel. You know where you have to find the rest of the story? You've got to turn all the way over to 2 Kings 9 to find out the rest of the story.

A man named Jehu is now king of Israel. Like many others before him had done, he came to power by killing the reigning king. When one of Elisha's prophets anointed Jehu some twenty years later, he gave Jehu a message from God to wipe out the house of Ahab once and for all (2 Kings 9:4–10). Jezebel still lived in the palace at Jezreel. There was one tiny fact that she didn't know. Twenty years earlier, Jehu had been there the day that Ahab had gone to take over Naboth's vineyard. He knew it was wrong because he knew the Word of the Lord. And if you read the story of Jehu, you know he was not what we would call a Sunday school-type person. He was a pretty tough customer. You didn't want to get on his bad side. But he was a far sight better than wicked Ahab. Though Jehu was kind of rough and wild and uncouth, he knew the difference between right and wrong. On one level at least, he wanted to do right in the eyes of the Lord. And he had never forgotten what Ahab had done to Naboth. So the Bible says he got in his chariot and he made a little trip.

"Then Jehu went to Jezreel" (2 King 9:30 NIV). That's the summer palace. This is where it all started. The former vineyard of Naboth was now a royal vegetable garden. "When Jezebel heard about it, she painted her eyes, arranged her hair and looked out of a window" (v. 30 NIV). She thought she was going to seduce Jehu. Wrong. He was not in the mood. As Jehu entered the gate, she called out, "Have you come in peace?" (v. 31 NIV). It's the last thing she ever said, except for "Oh no!" Jehu looked up and called out, "Who is on my side?" (v. 32 NIV). There were two or three eunuchs standing near Jezebel. They served Jezebel, they knew her for what she was, and they didn't like her. So Jehu said, "Boys, I got a job for you.

Grab that woman and throw her out." With pleasure, one imagines, they grabbed Jezebel; gave her the old one, two, three; and out the window she went, bouncing all the way down. Bam! She hit the ground hard. "They threw her down, and some of her blood spattered the wall and the horses as they trampled her underfoot" (v. 33 NIV). You know what this means? It means when they threw her body down, Jehu took his chariot and ran over her again and again and again until she was absolutely, completely, totally dead. She had hoof prints on her chest. She had chariot wheel marks on her legs. She was completely done for.

A little while later Jehu said, "We can't leave that mess out there. Somebody go get her and bury her." So he sent his servants out, and they came back and said, "Well, we've got good news and bad news. The good news is she is still dead. The bad news is there's not much left. The dogs have come and licked up the blood. They have destroyed her body. Nothing is left except her skull, her feet and her hands." We'll let Jehu have the final word:

"This is the word of the LORD that he spoke through his servant Elijah the Tishbite: On the plot of ground at Jezreel dogs will devour Jezebel's flesh" (v. 36 NIV).

The Moral of the Story

What a story. Elijah had been in heaven for ten years, but the word of the Lord came true. Let's focus on two important truths from this story.

First, God's patience will not last forever. Part of the gospel message is a message of judgment. The Lord is not slack as some people count slackness. He's not slow in the way some people count slowness. He is long-suffering and patient, not willing that any should perish but that all should come to repentance (cf. 2 Pet. 3:9). But there is a day of judgment coming for all of us. No one knows when that day will be, but there is a day for every man and woman and boy and girl. There's a day for every family, and there's a day for every nation. There is a day when God will finally say, "This far and no farther." God's patience will not last forever.

Do you remember when that guy with multicolored hair showed up at football games holding up John 3:16? We haven't seen him for a few years. He had rainbow-colored hair, and somehow he would get a seat right behind the goalposts. And just when they were about to kick an extra point, he would hold up a sign that read John 3:16. I had never given the matter any thought, but recently I read a comment along these lines. Why only hold up John 3:16, a verse the world likes because it speaks of God's love? What about John 3:18? "Whoever believes in him is not condemned, but whoever does not believe stands condemned already because he has not believed in the name of God's one and only Son" (NIV). That's also in the Bible. Our God is patient, but his patience does run out. You don't believe it? Just ask Ahab and Jezebel.

Second, God still looks for Elijahs who will stand up for him. We live in strange times. Morally confused times, days of religious and spiritual compromise. How we need a generation of men and women who will have the courage of their convictions and won't just deliver the good news but will have the courage to deliver the bad news too. We need someone to say to this dying generation, "Except you repent, you too will perish."

During the days of the English Reformation, there was a man by the name of Hugh Latimer who was a marvelous preacher of the gospel. He was so bold and outspoken that he ended up being burned at the stake. One day he was preaching before the king, and the king was nervous because everyone knew that Latimer was a loose cannon. He was an Elijah. He would say anything. And Latimer knew the king was nervous. People had said to him, "Now, Latimer, when you go speak before the king, be careful. Don't say anything that will make him upset." Latimer knew everybody was saying that and thinking that. And so in his sermon he started talking out loud to himself. "Latimer, Latimer, be careful what you say. King Henry is listening." And then he paused and said, "Latimer, Latimer, be careful what you say. The King of kings is listening."

Oh for some Elijahs who will care more for the King of kings than for the kings and queens of this dying world.

In all the world there are two groups and only two. You have Ahab and Jezebel, and you have Naboth and Elijah, and there's nothing in between. *Everyone who reads my words is in one of those two groups.* There's nobody in between. Ultimately you're either with Ahab and Jezebel, or you're with Naboth and Elijah. Who got the better deal? For a long time it looked like Ahab and Jezebel got the better deal. Today it often looks like the bad guys are winning. It often looks like those who flout the word of the Lord prosper. And in many places around the world—in China, Sudan, Afghanistan, Uzbekistan—it looks like God's people are taking it on the chin. Everybody gets to decide which team you want to be on. If you join Ahab and Jezebel, you can have worldly success, and the dogs will lick up your blood. Or you can stand with Naboth and Elijah.

Ahab and Jezebel.

Naboth and Elijah.

Which side are you on?

Chapter 12

S THERE NO GOD?

"Hell is truth seen too late."
Mortimer Zuckerman

This is the story of Elijah's last assignment.

God has one final job for his mountain man, and then he will take him home to heaven. The story begins this way: "After Ahab's death, Moab rebelled against Israel. Now Ahaziah . . ." (2 Kings 1:1–2 NIV). Ahaziah was Ahab's son. Ahab had two sons, and both of them rebelled against the Lord. When Ahab died, his older son Ahaziah ascended to the throne of Israel. Remember that Jezebel was still alive. She lived for many more years. She was really the effective ruler of Israel. But one of Ahab's sons was sitting on the throne. He would only be on the throne for two short years, and then he would be gone. And it's the story of how he died that occupies our attention today.

Now here's the problem. Ahaziah had fallen through the lattice of his upper room in Samaria and injured himself. *As far as kingly injuries go, this is a real bummer.* If the king injured himself on the battlefield, that would be a manly injury and an honorable way to die. But to fall off the second story through the latticework and hit the ground below, that's just embarrassing. It's definitely not something you want to publicize. We don't know how it happened. Did somebody push him? Did he stumble? Was he drunk? We don't know. When he hit the ground, he was evidently severely injured. And no one could help him. No one in all Israel could heal his injuries. So he thought to himself, *I need some help from above.* Only by *above* he wasn't thinking of the Lord God of Israel; he was thinking of someone else. "So he sent messengers, saying to them, 'Go and consult Baal-zebub, the god of Ekron, to see if I will recover from this injury'" (v. 2 NIV).

The name Baal-zebub appears only here in the Old Testament. Baal, of course, was the name of the false god that Jezebel had brought in. He was the god of the sun, the god of the storms, the god of fertility. He was the god of the pagan nations surrounding Israel. The rest of the name means what it sounds like. Zebub actually gives you the sound. Zzzzzebub, it means the buzzing of flies. Baal-zebub literally means "lord of the flies." Baal-zebub was the particular name for the god of the people of the region of Ekron, a city located on the Mediterranean Sea. It was one of the five major cities of the Philistines. When they offered sacrifices to Baal-zebub, the Philistines believed he could predict the future. To the extent it was true, it was the work of demons through this false god. That's why Ahaziah wanted to consult Baal-zebub. He wanted to know if he would get better or if he was going to die from his injuries.

There is only one catch to this story. Israel already had a God, the Lord God of Israel. Instead of turning to the true God, Ahaziah put his future in the hands of Baal-zebub.

Boo-Yah!

I pause here to comment that on one level we can understand Ahaziah's desire. *All of us would like to know the future.* We want to know what's going to happen tomorrow, the day after tomorrow, next week, next month, next year. Big corporations spend millions of dollars on consultants who can predict future business trends. If you have a loved one with cancer, you want to know what the future holds. If you have children, you constantly wonder (and sometimes worry) about the decisions they make. At this very moment I would like to know my own future. At least I think I would. Maybe I wouldn't be so happy if I knew it. Who knows?

If you are an investor, you'd like to know about the stock market. That's why people watch Jim Cramer give his stock picks on the TV show called *Mad Money*. People call in and shout "Boo-yah" to Cramer, and he shouts "Boo-yah" back. Then they say something like, "Jim, what do you think about Amalgamated Fruit Juice of North Dakota—AFJND?" He punches a button, and up comes the recent stock history of AFJND. Then he begins to shout about how the orange crop in North Dakota isn't good this year and how oranges grow better in Florida, but North Dakota wheat is looking good, but he thinks the stock is overpriced. "It's a dog! Dump that puppy." And he hits a button, and you hear a flushing sound. "I want you in United Onions. They're best of breed," he says. And then he goes to the next caller. It's all bang, bang, bang. And it's irresistible. It's mesmerizing. I'll grant that he's a good entertainer and knowledgeable. But there is something more at work here. Cramer is a guru, a genius at the stock market. Or so it seems. I'm not qualified to judge. But I watch because it's a good performance, and I want to know the future just as much as anyone else. And I don't even have any money in AFJND or United Onions either.

It becomes much more personal when you're wondering about your own health or the health of your spouse or your children. I have a friend whose wife is struggling with cancer that threatens to take her life. They are dear friends and some of the godliest people I have ever known. During a long battle with cancer that now stretches into a seventh year, I have never known her to utter a single word of complaint. Despite repeated rounds of chemotherapy that have sapped her strength, leaving her vulnerable to other diseases, she has continued to serve on the worship team of her church, and she has continued to take care of her family. Recently the doctors found that a certain tumor had started growing so they are trying some sort of powerful superdrug that has helped some patients. Her husband wrote an update that went to many friends. He signed it, "Waiting upon healing, holding onto hope."

You want to know if your children are going to get married, and if so, who's the lucky person going to be? Will they be happy? Will it last? And how soon will they bring the grandchildren over? You think about your own career and wonder, "Lord, is this what I'm supposed to be doing for the rest of my life? If not, would you please let me know somehow?" That's perfectly understandable. We all wonder about things like that. "Lord, I have my dreams and my concerns. I have things that weigh heavily on my heart. Lord, what is my own future? Show me the way I should go."

Crossing Over

I don't criticize Ahaziah for wanting to know if he would recover. That's natural. *But he went to the wrong place.* That would prove to be a fatal mistake. We should not be surprised because when people get desperate, they will turn to any source that promises them help. You talk to a friend on the phone. You call the psychic hotline. You look at your horoscope. You might even call a medium, a spiritualist. We tend to think of mediums as if they were like the wicked witch in *The Wizard of* Oz. Today's mediums look like you and me.

A few times I have watched a TV show hosted by a young man who looks like the guy next door. Pleasant. Nice looking. Well dressed but not overdressed. Friendly smile. Casual demeanor. He looks like he might have been a high school quarterback. He looks like the All-American guy. The kind of neighbor anyone would want to have. He has even written a book about praying the rosary. You say to yourself, "A good Catholic boy." And oh yes, he claims to be able to contact your dead relatives. People pay huge money to go to group sessions where he claims to receive messages from someone who has "passed." He's good at it too. Very good. Talks fast, makes quick word associations, claims to hear voices or get images from the "other side." Always the message from the dead is, "We're doing good. Don't worry about us. You're doing well and we love you." Very comforting.

He calls himself a medium and claims to be a spiritist with an uncanny ability to foretell the future and to communicate with the dead. I understand why people go to him because he looks as normal as anybody you'll ever meet. Please understand. The desire to know the future is not wrong in itself. What's wrong is going to the wrong place. People who go to mediums are drinking from a polluted fountain, and what they get will not be from God. What they get will be demonically inspired poison that will destroy their souls.

Elijah's Final Message

Things haven't changed much in three thousand years. Ahaziah's great mistake was going to the wrong place. So he sent his messengers down to Ekron. There they were going to somehow get in touch with Baal-zebub to find out if the king would recover from his injuries. We pick up the story again in verse 3: "But the angel of the LORD said to Elijah the Tishbite, 'Go up and meet the messengers of the king of Samaria and ask them, "Is it because there is no God in Israel that you are going off to consult Baal-zebub, the god of Ekron?"'" (NIV).

Notice the phrase *"go up."* Older translations use the word *arise*. Same as when God told him to confront Ahab over the murder of Naboth. "Arise." "Get up, Elijah. I've got a job for you to do." Go and ask him one question: "Is there no God in Israel?" Is there no Lord God Almighty in Israel that you should go down to the pagans and you should ask the pagan god about the future? Now comes the bad news for Ahaziah: "You will not leave the bed you are lying on. You will certainly die!" (v. 4 NIV).

Notice the next phrase: "So Elijah went." That's all it says. God gave him the message, and Elijah delivered it. Bam! Just like the other times. He shows up out of nowhere, gives the message, and disappears. Evidently the messengers were so disconcerted that they never made it to Ekron. They went back to the king with this report: "'A man came to meet us,' they replied. 'And he said to us, "Go back to the king who sent you and tell him, 'This is what the LORD says: Is it because there is no God in Israel that you are sending men to consult Baal-zebub, the god of Ekron? Therefore you will not leave the bed you are lying on. You will certainly die!'"'" (v. 6 NIV).

So the king wants to know who dared give such a negative message. I love their answer because it's clear they have no idea who he is. They describe Elijah this way: "He was a man with a garment of hair and with a leather belt around his waist" (v. 8 NIV). According to L. L. Bean this is what the well-dressed mountain man should always be wearing. The king says, "I know that fellow. That was Elijah the Tishbite."

Lost People Watch Us

Think about this for a moment. The king knew Elijah. Why? Because Elijah had dealt with his father Ahab. *Lost people watch us more than we know.* Lost people pay more attention to us than we ever dream. Lost people know more than we think they do. More than anything else, lost people know whether we know God. They watch us to see if we're the real deal. They watch us from a distance. Your coworkers are watching you. Your neighbors are watching you. Your unsaved relatives are watching you. They may not say much to you. You may not be aware of it. You may not even hear from them for years. But the day will come when you're going to find out that some people were watching you all the time and drawing conclusions about your faith, your integrity, and your honesty. And they are drawing conclusions about the reality of your faith in God.

I believe God often gives lost people amazing insight into the Christians around them. That is to say I believe God's Spirit gives unsaved people the ability to penetrate to the core of who we are. If you go to lost people and give them a doctrinal exam, they would flunk it. But if you took most lost people and put a group of Christians they know in front of them, I believe most lost people would without any trouble at all be able to say, "He's for real, she's for real, and those two in the back, I don't see anything in them at all." They may not understand the Trinity or total depravity, and the whole concept of the premillennial return of Christ may be a mystery to them, but lost people can tell the difference between reality and fakery. If you doubt that, just ask some of your unsaved friends, "What do you see when you look at me?" You might be surprised at the answer.

So the king knew. He said, "That was Elijah the Tishbite."

Now the king sends out some men to capture Elijah. He sends out a captain with his company of fifty men. "The captain went up to Elijah, who was sitting on the top of a hill" (v. 9 NIV). I love that because Elijah is just sitting up there on the top of the hill, talking to the Lord, catching some rays, enjoying the day. He's not hiding this time. He's out in the open where anybody can see him. And the captain of the fifty says, "Man of God, the king says, 'Come down'." What do you think the king wants? The king wants to throw him in jail. Elijah says, "If I am a man of God, may fire come down from heaven and consume you and your fifty men" (v. 10 NIV). I'm sure that's the last thing the captain of the fifty wanted to hear. As a matter of fact, it *was* the last thing he heard because the next sentence says, "Then fire fell from heaven and consumed the captain and his men" (v. 10 NIV).

Evidently the king was a slow learner because he sent another captain with his fifty men to capture Elijah. Same story, second verse.

"'Man of God, this is what the king says, "Come down at once!"'" 'If I am a man of God,' Elijah replied, 'may fire come down from heaven and consume you and your fifty men!' Then the fire of God fell from heaven and consumed him and his fifty men" (vv. 11–12 NIV).

Where Could I Go but to the Lord?

Bam! Just like that, down came the fire consuming the second captain and the second fifty men. So the king sent a third captain with his fifty men. I doubt they were volunteers. I imagine the captain had to use a little forceful persuasion. The third captain, who was smarter than the king, decided he didn't want to end up in flames. "This third captain went up and fell on his knees before Elijah. 'Man of God,' he begged, 'please have respect for my life and the lives of these fifty men, your servants! See, fire has fallen from heaven and consumed the first two captains and all their men. But now have respect for my life!'" (vv. 13–14 NIV).

The angel of the Lord told Elijah to go with him to see the king. Earlier he had stood before Ahab the father; now he stands before Ahaziah the son. It took a certain amount of courage to do that because Ahaziah is sick. He's now been told by the prophet he's going to die. A hundred of his soldiers have died, consumed by fire. I'm sure he's in a foul mood. I am sure Elijah knew that the king might try to put him to death at any moment. What do you think Elijah did? He didn't wait for Ahaziah to say a word.

"This is what the LORD says: Is it because there is no God in Israel for you to consult that you have sent messengers to consult Baal-zebub, the god of Ekron? Because you have done this, you

will never leave the bed you are lying on. You will certainly die!"
(v. 16 NIV).

Is there no God in Israel? What a question for all of us!

Is there no God in your town?

Is there no God in your church?

Is there no God in your family?

Is there no God in your marriage?

Is there no God in your life?

Is there no God to whom you can go in the time of trouble?

Abraham Lincoln said, "I have been driven many times to my knees by the overwhelming thought that I had nowhere else to go."

So the king died just as Elijah said he would. There are no details because it doesn't matter. He's gone. The only thing that really matters is the first part of verse 17. "So he died, according to the word of the LORD."

A Personal View of Death

I have been closely touched by death a handful of times in my life. When I was in junior high school, a close friend came home sick from a youth group outing on Saturday afternoon. Overnight his condition worsened. The next morning he died. It shook me up because he and I used to wrestle in his front yard. Then we would go inside, sit on the sofa, and read comic books. He'd come to my house sometimes, and we'd fool around together. We were just typical good friends. And then he died. The whole school was dismissed for his funeral. I remember that the church sanctuary was packed with people. The casket was open in the front. Some of my friends went down front to look at him. I remember standing at the back of that crowded sanctuary and seeing the outline of his face above the edge of the coffin. He was the first dead person I had ever seen. I was too scared to go up for a closer look.

I was in college when my grandmother died. She was in her eighties and had been sick for some time so it came as no surprise. I drove through the night from Chattanooga to Nashville to Memphis and down to Oxford to attend the funeral service. They took me in to see her. Someone commented, "They did a good job, didn't they?" In the hallway my relatives were standing round laughing, talking, joking, sipping drinks. Only one aunt seemed concerned at all. I remember that it seemed rather bizarre, drinking cocktails at a funeral home.

But death remained shadowy for me until my father died in 1974. He was a popular surgeon in the small town in Alabama where I grew up. To use an old-timey expression, he took sick and died. No other event has affected my life like the death of my father. It took me a long time to deal with the reality that whenever I went home from now on, he wouldn't be there to greet me.

Run the clock forward a bit over twenty years to the day when my friend Len Hoppe died. He was an elder in the church in Oak Park, a dear friend and a man of enormous faith who fervently believed God would heal him. Nine days after his cancer surgery, he died. We buried him on a bitterly cold day in Chicago. Gary Olson and I prayed with Len before his surgery. Then Gary spoke at Len's funeral and said, "I can almost hear Len talking to me from heaven saying, 'Gary, get on up here. It's great.'" Three years later Gary would indeed "get on up there" when he died suddenly while working out at the high school. I still remember the shock of getting the phone call saying he had collapsed. And I remember standing by his body in the hospital emergency room. His death hit me hard in ways that I still find difficult to explain almost seven years later.

"Ray, Take a Good Look"

Then my mother died several years ago. I had the honor of speaking at her graveside service where we buried her next to my father. While I was standing there, I had a surreal personal experience. Perhaps it happened partly because I was a bit under the weather; perhaps it was seeing so many old friends after three decades; perhaps it was because we were burying my mother and my father side by side. It was as if there was a "wrinkle in time" and the twenty-nine years since my father died had suddenly been swallowed up. They just disappeared for a moment. I was in my early twenties when Dad died; I'm in my early fifties now. Most of the family friends who came to the graveside service had been at my father's funeral twenty-nine years earlier. Most of them were in their early fifties then; most are in their late seventies or early eighties now. It seemed as if the three decades in between had just disappeared. All this passed through my mind in a flash while I was speaking. I could reach out and touch my mother's coffin. I was standing three feet from where we buried my father. It was as if we buried my father last week, we were burying my mother this week, and next week someone would bury me. I had a tremendous sense of my own mortality, of the quickly passing years. It seemed as if the Lord whispered in my ear, "Ray, take a good look. This is where you will be someday." And that day will come sooner than I think.

Yesterday my father died.

Today my mother died.

Tomorrow I will die.

Decades may pass between those events, but all are certain to happen. I cannot totally explain what I experienced that day, yet it was profound to me, and I am still thinking about it. It was a revelation of my own weakness, my humanity, my frailty, a reminder that "dust thou art, to the dust thou shalt return." This is always true for all of us, but often we live as if we don't believe it.

I am not sure how many funerals I have conducted over the years. But I vividly remember my first funeral after becoming pastor of a church in Downey, California. I was fresh out of seminary, a newly minted pastor; and not long after I arrived, I was asked to do a funeral service for a man I had never met. I was young and inexperienced and thought to say a few words of comfort. I fumbled my way through the ceremony and came to the closing prayer. When I got to the part about the resurrection of the dead, the words stuck in my throat. I could barely finish my prayer. I went back home frustrated and embarrassed. What had gone wrong? Then it hit me. I wasn't sure I believed in the resurrection of the dead. Up until then, it had all been theoretical. But now I had come face-to-face with death, and all my brave words seemed so hollow.

Fear Factor

Death has a way of doing that to us. It shocks us, scares us, sobers us up. Even the most suave and debonair young man is forced to stand with open mouth and wide eyes before an open casket. Cemeteries aren't much better. Something about that fresh mound of dirt makes us shudder. Something makes us drive faster past a cemetery late at night lest we accidentally shine our lights on a tombstone. Death makes us realize our mortality, our weakness. Death frightens us because we instinctively know that someday we too shall die. Most of all, death makes us think. It makes us think about our own lives, our priorities, our goals, ourselves. And we hate to think about that. So we avoid death at all costs. We avoid death because we don't want to think about life.

There are so many fears related to the fear of death:

We fear dying alone.
We fear dying a painful death.
We fear what may happen after we die.
We fear leaving our loved ones behind.
We fear the unknown, and death is the ultimate unknown.
We fear death because of our sins.
We fear standing before God after we die.

And so we do whatever we can to avoid death at all costs. We change the subject, we live as if we were never going to die, we drink ourselves senseless, we turn to sex to keep us occupied, we bury ourselves in our work, and we try our best not to think about the moment of our own death. Martin Luther said we should live with the day of our death constantly before our eyes. That way we won't be surprised when the day finally comes. And come it will. Death is no respecter of persons. The statistics are awesome to contemplate:

One out of every one person will die someday. No one gets a free pass.

Death *is* a problem. It was a problem in Bible times, and it's still a problem today. Death is the great leveler, the ultimate equalizer. Donald Trump will die someday, and so will the poorest man in the poorest village in Bangladesh. "It is appointed unto men once to die" (Heb. 9:27 KJV). Thus says the Lord. And that's an appointment no one can skip and no one can postpone.

Peter Blakemore

Death comes to all of us sooner or later. I spent a week preaching at Gull Lake Conference Center in Michigan. Twice I heard the executive director say, "Hell is hot; life is short." What is your life? It is a vapor that appears for a while and then vanishes away. Moses prayed, "Teach us to number our days aright, that we may gain a heart of wisdom" (Ps. 90:12 NIV).

Shortly before my friend Peter Blakemore died, I saw him for the last time at a pastor's prayer meeting on the National Day of Prayer. I hadn't seen Peter in a while because he had been struggling with cancer. I knew he had been through an awful ordeal, but I had no idea how bad it was. When I arrived at the prayer meeting, I knew almost everyone there because they all pastored churches in the same area. There was one man sitting in a wheelchair with two young men around him. Because his back was to me, I didn't know who it was till I sat down in the circle. Then I saw it was my friend Peter Blakemore. Peter was the pastor of the Harrison Street Bible Church in Oak Park. Before Peter was the pastor, his father had pastored that church for over thirty years. Except for his years in college and graduate school, Peter spent his whole life in Oak Park. When he completed his education, he came back to Oak Park to join his father at Harrison

Street Bible Church. And when his father died, he took over the pastorate in his father's stead. Peter Blakemore was one of the gentlest, kindest, most gracious men I have ever known. He was about forty years old when he died. He left behind a wife and seven children. He was stricken with an extremely rare form of cancer. They sent samples to various places around the country, hoping to find a cure. He had gone through a variety of treatments but nothing worked. The cancer finally had taken over his body with a vengeance. And there he was at the National Day of Prayer with two of his sons.

We bowed our heads; and as we prayed, I noticed a strange sound, a sort of rubbing or thumping in a rhythmic fashion. I didn't know what it was. Peter Blakemore was the last one to pray that day. And he said, "Lord, you know I've asked you to heal me of this cancer. And if you do heal me, I will stand up and give you the glory. But if you decide to take me home to heaven, Lord, I'm going to be faithful to you by my life and by my death so that in all things you might be glorified."

When the prayer meeting was over, almost everybody left the room. There were just four of us left—Peter, his two sons, and me. We talked for a while. He told me a little bit about the treatments. Just recently they had heard from the doctors that there was a new kind of tumor growing in his lungs, and the doctors couldn't even figure out what it was. They said it's one of two things. If it's one thing, you're going to live one to three weeks. If it's another thing, you're going to live two or three months. The tumor had grown inside his lungs to the point that it had broken two or three of his ribs. While he was praying, he was hunched over in the wheelchair. The rhythmic thump I heard was the sound of his oldest son rubbing his father's back to lessen the pain a little bit.

Peter told me that the previous Sunday he had preached at his own church for the first time in eight weeks. He preached from the wheelchair on Romans 11:33, "Oh, the depth of the riches of the wisdom and knowledge of God! How unsearchable his judgments, and his paths beyond tracing out!" (NIV). "Do you know what that means, Ray?" Peter said it was like tracing the stars in the skies. When you look up at night and see a star, you know that it is on a path, but if you just look at it, all you can do is see where it is now. You can't really tell where it has come from or where it's going to go. And he said, "So it is with the Lord. No one can tell where he started out. No one can tell where he's going to go. All you know is he's right there and you're right there with him, and the future is in his hands." Then he added, "I told my people last Sunday, 'I have shown you how to live. I'm now going to show you how to die.'" These were his final words to me: "All my life I've preached about the grace of God. I've had a hard time getting people to listen. Now I don't have any trouble because they've seen the grace of God at work in my life."

We said farewell, and his sons wheeled him out of the room. It was the last time I would see him alive. Two or three weeks later he passed from this life into the presence of the Lord Jesus Christ. I thought about what he said, and I've thought about it many times since then. Who can trace the path of the Lord? You can't. I can't. No one can. It is enough to know that we belong to him. He knows what he's doing. He knows where we are. And when it's all over, we will be exactly where he wants us to be, with him forever in heaven.

Nada. Zip. Zero.

Sometimes I think about my own death. It's not something I look forward to. I'd prefer to live a while longer if the Lord allows it. And if I've got to go, I'd just as soon it be in my sleep peacefully. But there are no guarantees, none at all, except that unless the Lord returns in my lifetime, I'll certainly die someday. I might die in a fiery crash, or I might have a heart attack, or I might waste away with some dread disease. I might be the victim of a crime. Or I might grow old and simply slip away slowly. Though I know a few things about life, about the circumstances of my own death I have no knowledge whatsoever. None at all, except for this. I know what will happen the moment I die. I'm totally certain about that. With all my heart I believe that I will see the Lord Jesus Christ, and he will welcome me into heaven. I do not believe I "deserve" to go to heaven or that I could ever "earn" eternal life. What an empty pipe dream that is. When I go to heaven, it will be because Jesus takes me there. And when he takes me there, it will be because his blood has covered all my sins, and he has given me his own perfect righteousness.

If I show up at the gates of heaven talking about how good I've been, I'm in real trouble. First of all, I haven't been all that good. Too many sins come crowding into my memory, and those are only the ones I can remember. I testify that I am a sinner through and through; and left to myself, I don't have a chance of going to heaven.

Nada.

Zip.

Zero.

Not going to make it.

And if I start talking about my own paltry good works, which are far too few to matter, the Lord will turn me away, and I will spend eternity in hell. That's not something I care to contemplate, but I believe hell is a real place and that some people will be there forever, separated from God for eternity times eternity times eternity. So when my time comes to die, I'd better not be spouting any nonsense about how good Ray Pritchard has been. That will only get me in big trouble. What, then, can I say?

Consider these words from the Heidelberg Catechism, written in 1563.[1] Here is how it begins:

Question 1: What is your only comfort in life and in death?

Answer: That I am not my own, but belong with body and soul, both in life and in death, to my faithful Savior Jesus Christ. He has fully paid for all my sins with His precious blood, and has set me free from all the power of the devil. He also preserves me in such a way that without the will of my heavenly Father not a hair can fall from my head; indeed, all things must work together for my salvation. Therefore, by His Holy Spirit He also assures me of eternal life and makes me heartily willing and ready from now on to live for Him.

That's the sort of statement every Christian should memorize. Why don't you stop right now and read it out loud? It will do your soul good to say those words. Just stop for a moment and read it aloud. You might want to write it down and put it on your mirror so you can say it every morning.

For many people, death is a painful passing from this life into the life to come. The process of dying can be excruciating. So

I don't necessarily look forward to my own death. But I can say this plainly: I'm not afraid to die. If you find out tomorrow morning that during the night I died, be assured that I was ready to go. It's not because I'm some kind of *Terminator/Die Hard*/John Wayne-type who can look death in the face and laugh. And it's not because I'm prayed up or because my life makes me a holy man. I am ready to die because I know Jesus Christ and he has freed me from the fear of death.

Waking Up in Heaven

Peter Marshall tells the story of a young boy about four years old who had a terminal disease. At first he was simply sick and in bed and didn't understand his condition, but eventually he realized that he wasn't going to get better and would never again play with his friends. One morning he asked his mother, "Am I going to die?" And she said, "Yes, dear." "Mommy, what is death like? Will it hurt?" The mother ran out of the room to the kitchen and leaned against the refrigerator, her knuckles gripped white to keep from crying. She prayed and asked the Lord to give her an answer for her son.

Suddenly an idea came, and she went back to his room and sat down on the bed. "Do you remember how you used to play outside all day, and when you came inside at night, you were so tired you just fell down on the couch and slept? In the morning you woke up in your own bed. During the night your father would come along and pick you up and carry you to your own bed. That's what death is like. One night you lie down and go to sleep and your heavenly Father picks you up and carries you to your own bed. In the morning when you wake up, you're in your own room in heaven." The little boy smiled and nodded. And several weeks later he died peacefully. That's what death is like for the Christian. Satan's hold is broken. The fear is taken away. Jesus came to break the bondage of death.

After Gary Olson died a few years ago, someone sent me the words to a hymn written in 1681 by Richard Baxter called "Lord, It Belongs Not to My Care." I printed the words and carried them with me for many months and found in them consolation for my soul. I found that paper recently as I was unpacking a box. The words have an enormous power. Baxter added this note when he published the hymn in 1681: "This covenant my dear wife in her former sickness subscribed with a cheerful will."[2]

> Lord, it belongs not to my care
> Whether I die or live;
> To love and serve Thee is my share,
> And this Thy grace must give.
> If life be long, I will be glad,
> That I may long obey;
> If short, yet why should I be sad
> To soar to endless day?
> Christ leads us through no darker rooms
> Than He went through before;
> He that unto God's kingdom comes
> Must enter by this door.
> Come, Lord, when grace hath made me meet
> Thy blessed face to see;
> For if Thy work on earth be sweet
> What will Thy glory be!
> My knowledge of that life is small,
> The eye of faith is dim;
> But 'tis enough that Christ knows all,
> And I shall be with Him.

"You're Looking in the Wrong Place"

Let me return for a moment to the first funeral service I conducted as a pastor when I stumbled through the prayer and later realized that the reality of death had overwhelmed my faith in the resurrection of the saints. Out of that experience I began to pray, and it seemed as if God said to me, "Son, you're looking in the wrong place." There is indeed a grave that's empty, but it's over on the other side of the world, outside Jerusalem, carved into a mountainside. That tomb is empty, and it's been empty for two thousand years.

Several years ago I visited the Holy Land for the first time. During our visit to Jerusalem, we spent an hour at the garden tomb, the spot believed by many to be the actual burial place of Jesus. It is located next to Gordon's Calvary, that strange rock outcropping that appears to be worn into the shape of a skull. We know it was used as a burial site in Jesus' day. Many believe it was the spot of the crucifixion. The garden tomb is located about a hundred yards from Gordon's Calvary and is in fact the spot of a beautiful garden built over an ancient Roman aqueduct. To your left as you enter is a typical first-century tomb dug into the hillside. A trench in front of the opening was apparently designed for the massive stone that once covered the entrance.

Because the opening is very small, I had to duck to go inside. For a few seconds you see nothing until your eyes adjust to the darkness. Then you can easily make out the two chambers. Visitors stand in the mourners' chamber. A wrought-iron fence protects the chamber where the body was laid. You soon notice that the burial chamber was originally designed for two bodies. However one ledge was never finished for some reason. The other one was. It appears to be designed for a person slightly less than six feet tall.

As I looked around the burial chamber, I could see faint markings left by Christian pilgrims from earlier centuries. After a few seconds another thought enters the mind. There is no body to be found in this tomb. Whoever was buried there evidently left a long time ago. The garden tomb is empty!

As you exit back into the sunlight, your eyes fasten upon a wooden sign: "Why seek ye the living among the dead? He is not here, for he is risen, as he said."

"Look What I Did for My Son"

We look at our loved ones dying and wonder if the resurrection can be true. But that's backward. God says, "Look what I did for my Son. Will I do any less for those who put their trust in him?" Put simply: We do not believe in the resurrection of the dead because of anything we can see with our eyes; everything we see argues against it. People die all the time. There hasn't been a resurrection in a long, long time. But that doesn't matter. We believe in the resurrection of the saints because we believe in the resurrection of Jesus. "For since we believe that Jesus died and rose again, even so, through Jesus, God will bring with him those who have fallen asleep" (1 Thess. 4:14).

What's going to happen today or tomorrow? I don't know. What's going to happen next week or next month? I don't know. What's going to happen next year or ten years from now? I don't know. But I know someone who does.

Is there no God in Israel? Yes, there is. And he's my God too. I don't know what the future holds, but I know who holds the future.

And we can trust him.

Chapter 13

HARIOTS OF FIRE

"It does not matter whether or not people understand us or think we are even sane as long as we are true to God. Obedience to him is the important thing."

THEODORE EPP

What would you do if you knew that you were going to die today?

What if you knew with absolute certainty that today was going to be your last day on earth? Suppose you had less than twenty-four hours to live. What would you do? Where would you go? How would you spend your last few hours on planet Earth? If you knew you were going to die today, what would you do? Where would you go? Would you stay where you are right now, or would you hop on a plane and go see someone you love? Would you pick up the phone and call a few people? If you did, whom would you call? What would you say?

It's good to think about questions like this from time to time. Martin Luther said that we should live every day with the day of our death always before us, like a billboard we see everywhere we turn. In his book *The Seven Secrets of Highly Effective People*, Steven Covey talks about living with the end in view. That's a great biblical principle—to live today as if it were your last day. Martyred missionary Jim Elliott said he wanted to live so that when it came time to die, there would be nothing else he needed to do but die.

Let's sharpen the question just a bit. Suppose you had just thirty seconds to live. Perhaps you've been injured in a terrible car accident, or perhaps you're dying in a hospital, and you know the end is near. Your family is gathered around you, waiting for your final words. Suppose you have thirty seconds, and then you're gone. What would you say? How would you sum up all that was important to you? I thought about that for a while and wondered what I would say to my three sons. It didn't take me long to come up with an answer. In my final thirty seconds, I would say four things to my boys:

1. Take care of your mother.
2. Love each other.
3. Marry Christian wives.
4. Serve Jesus Christ forever.

That's it. Take care of your mother, love each other, marry Christian wives, and serve Jesus Christ forever. If my boys did all that, then I would die a happy man. That summarizes everything I've tried to live for.

I have a friend who served in combat in Vietnam. He was captured by the North Vietnamese, shot in the feet, and escaped by crawling out of the prison camp on his hands and knees. He knows all about war because he's seen men die in battle. Not long ago he told me that Americans are afraid to die. He wasn't talking about the brave men and women who serve in our armed forces. They lay their lives on the line every day, and they do it without asking for sympathy. They do it because it is their job and because they believe in what America stands for. That's not what my friend meant. He meant that ordinary Americans are afraid to die. He told me a few years ago, and he said it again after a terrorist attack in London. He said the difference between us and the terrorists is that we're afraid to die and they're not.

We were sitting on a park bench in the center of a beautiful city on a lovely summer day. "Look at all we've got." I saw happy couples strolling together hand in hand and young people stretched out on the grass. "We think we're already living in heaven. We think we've already got the best of all possible worlds. Why would anyone want to leave this?" Compare that to where the terrorists come from. No wonder they're not afraid to die. Americans are afraid to die precisely as a result of our own material prosperity. And because we've lost our confidence that there is another world beyond this one. Peggy Noonan explains it this way: "Our ancestors believed in two worlds, and understood this to be the solitary, poor, nasty, brutish and short one. We are the first generations of man that actually expected to find happiness here on earth, and our search for it has caused such unhappiness."[1]

That's a fairly accurate assessment of our whole society. *And in some ways it's true of the church as well.* Even inside the church we get a little bit squeamish talking about death. You're never going to say to your friends, "Hey, I've got some pizza. You bring the Coke. Come on over to my house; we're going to talk about death on Friday night." You're not going to say that because if you do, nobody's going to come. Nobody wants to talk about death. But in the old days when life was harder, people thought a lot more about death. John Wesley, the founder of the Methodist movement, used to say about his people, "Our people die well." *In earlier generations Christians talked about death a lot more than we do now.* The Puritans actually wrote books to help one another learn how to die well. Dying well was considered to be a Christian virtue.

What if I knew how many days I had left on this earth? What difference would it make to me?

I wouldn't waste so much time on trivial things.

I would set two or three goals and work like crazy to see them accomplished.

I wouldn't get angry so easily or hold a grudge so long.

I would take time to hug my boys at least once a day.

I wouldn't spend so much time watching television.

I would say, "I love you," more often than I do.

I wouldn't complain about spinach or tuna casserole or time spent window shopping at the mall.

I would write more letters.

I wouldn't worry about most of the things that currently bother me.

I wouldn't let pressure build up in the relationships that matter the most to me.

I would be quick to ask forgiveness when I hurt someone.

I wouldn't get disappointed when other people let me down.

I would pray every day for the love of Jesus to shine through my life.

I wouldn't put off saying "thank you" to others.

I would spend more time with Marlene and my boys because soon enough my time with them will be over.

I would pray more, love more, laugh more, simplify my life, rearrange my priorities, fret less, and concentrate on the things that really matter.

But if that's the way I would live then, why don't I live that way now? "We're all terminal," a friend reminded me. "Some of us just find out sooner than others."

So what would you do if today were your last day on earth? Where would you go? What would you do? Whom would you talk to? And what would you say?

Elijah's Last Day

And that brings us to the last chapter in Elijah's story. *From 2 Kings 2 we learn how a man of God leaves this earth well.* Elijah doesn't die, but the way he spends his last day is a message to us all.

We started our journey with Elijah in the mountains. From the mountains we went before the king. Then we went with Elijah to the brook, and after the brook we went to the widow of Zarephath. There we stayed with Elijah while miracles continued to happen. From there we climbed Mount Carmel with Elijah where he faced down the prophets of Baal. And after he left Mount Carmel, we followed him into the desert and then into a cave on Mount Horeb. We watched as he called Elisha in dramatic fashion. Then we went with Elijah as he stood before King Ahaziah. Now we've come to the final bend in the road, the last installment of his amazing life story.

On the last day of Elijah's earthly life, he does a lot of walking. He starts in Samaria and goes to Gilgal. From Gilgal he goes to Bethel. From Bethel he goes down to Jericho. From Jericho he goes to the east side of the Jordan River. His final walk takes him back to the hills and ravines of his boyhood. God's mountain man returns to the mountains from whence he came. Amid those lonely rocky hills and deep gullies, the prophet prepares to meet the Lord. Depending on the roads you take, that's at least forty to fifty-five miles. That's quite a bit of walking in one day. So whatever else you want to say, don't say Elijah was out of shape. He was obviously in excellent shape. Don't say he was taken to heaven because he was old and tired and worn out because Elijah still had plenty of vitality on his last day. He took this long walk because God had told him today is going to be the day.

Do you believe God sometimes gives his children a little advance notice that heaven is not far away? I do. I don't think he does it in every case. But I imagine most of us could tell a story of a saint of God who had some premonition that heaven was not far away. We hear stories of angels singing, of bright lights, of the vision of the glory of Christ. While I don't think we should be gullible and believe everything people say, I don't think that we should discount all those stories. Before he died, Stephen had a vision of heaven (Acts 7:55–56). *I believe that sometimes God allows us to hear the sound of the chariot swinging low to carry us home.* God in his grace sometimes allows his children to know that the day has arrived.

It's also clear that Elisha, his young protégé, also knew this was the final day. And it's clear that God had told the company of the prophets in these different towns. That explains why Elijah would do all that walking on his last day. It also answers a question that has been left hanging in the air. What was Elijah doing during those long stretches when he suddenly disappeared from view? Now we know the answer. *Elijah had obviously spent a great deal of his time building into other people.* In Gilgal and Bethel and Jericho (and probably other cities and towns as well), Elijah had set up little hometown seminaries where prophets could be trained for the ministry. He was the senior professor of practical theology at every extension campus of ITS—Israel Theological Seminary. This was distance learning in reverse. Instead of the young prophets coming to him, he came to them, teaching them how to walk with God, how to understand God's Word, how to preach, and how to lead others. In short, he did exactly what Paul instructed Timothy to do, "Teach others also." He understood that his greatest gift to the nation would be to multiply himself by leaving behind a crop of young men who could carry on his work after he was gone. One man could only do so much, but one man who poured himself into dozens of younger men could start a movement that might one day ignite a revolution that could overthrow Baal worship once and for all. Here is the ultimate argument for Christian education. We pass along what we know to the up-and-coming generation precisely because we know we won't be here forever. We do it so that our work will not end when we do, but in the providence of God, while we sink into the dust of the earth, God's truth goes marching on.

These young prophets loved Elijah and looked to him as their guide, mentor, hero, and friend. In Gilgal and Bethel and Jericho, everywhere he went that last day, the school of the prophets was dismissed. The young prophets who were trained by the older prophets came out to see the man of God as he made his farewell tour. God had not only told Elijah and Elisha; he also told the other prophets in Israel, "The man of God is going home today."

I think that Elijah knew that today was the day. I don't think he knew exactly when it was going to happen or where or how. I don't know that he had any inkling of being carried to heaven in a whirlwind. So Elijah now has Elisha with him. When he comes to Gilgal, he says, "Stay here." And Elisha says, "No, I'm going with you." When he comes to Bethel, he says, "Stay here." Elisha says, "No, I'm going with you." When he comes to Jericho, he says, "Stay here." "No, I'm going with you." When he comes to the Jordan he says, "Stay here." "No, I'm going with you." It was a test of loyalty and a test of tenacity. It was Elijah's way of saying to his man, *"I'm about to leave you. Can you handle it?"* And Elisha is saying to his mentor, *"Wherever you go I will go. I will be with you to the very end."* It's a touching picture of the older man and the younger man and the final test of loyalty.

So he spent his final day with Elisha, and he spent his time greeting and saying farewell to the young prophets who looked up to him as a hero and a mentor.

There is no sense of panic here. Elijah was not afraid; Elisha was not afraid. There's no sense of fear or dread, just a sense of being completely in God's hands.

Elijah's Last Words

When they came to the Jordan River, Elijah took his cloak, rolled it up, and struck the water. The water parted, showing yet one more time how Elijah and Moses were both filled with the Spirit of God. Just before Elijah left for heaven, he turned and said to his young friend, "What can I do for you? Before I go, do you have any last requests?" And Elisha said, "Let me inherit a double portion of your spirit" (2 Kings 2:9 NIV). Some people have criticized Elisha for making such a request, but I think they are misguided. Actually when Elisha asked for a double portion of Elijah's spirit, he was revealing the priorities of his life.

You find out what makes a man tick at a moment like this. Donald Trump says to you, "What can I do for you?" So you say, "Give me a wheelbarrow full of your money." He'll never miss it, he's got so much. You might say to somebody else, "Give me your contact list." You might say to somebody else, "Give me your business." "Give me your company." "Give me your network." "Give me your car." "Give me your home." "Give me your clothes." "Give me your stocks." "Give me your cattle." "Give me your farm." "Give me your family." "Give me your books."

Elisha asked only for a double portion of Elijah's spirit. *In the Old Testament the oldest son received a double portion of his father's estate.* Elisha was not literally the physical son of Elijah, but he was his spiritual son. So as the oldest son spiritually he was asking, "Oh my father, give me what belongs to me spiritually. Grant me a double portion of your spirit." Why did he ask for that? *Those were hard days in the nation of Israel, and soon matters would get worse.* Instead of getting better in the days of Elisha, the people continued to turn away from God. Elisha knew that in order for him to serve the Lord in the hard, difficult days ahead, he needed the same courage and the same resolve and the same fortitude and the same boldness that his master had had. He wanted the same spirit that Elijah had on top of Mount Carmel. He wanted the same spirit that caused him to go before Ahab in the first place. He wanted the same spirit that Elijah had had when he faced down Ahaziah. He wanted that, and he knew he needed it. God bless Elisha for realizing the need in his own life.

Elijah said back to him, "You have asked a difficult thing" (v. 10 NIV). It was a gift only God could give. Then he added an important condition: "If you see me when I am taken from you, it will be yours—otherwise not" (v. 10 NIV).

Now we come to the end of Elijah's earthly life. "As they were walking along and talking together, suddenly a chariot of fire and horses of fire appeared" (v. 11 NIV). Those are military images. The horses and the chariot were symbols of battle. *Elijah was a warrior for God.* It was a sign and a symbol that there was a battle raging for the hearts of people of Israel. It meant that a warrior was about to come home to God. It's a symbol of the kind of life Elijah has led. "Elijah went up to heaven in a whirlwind" (v. 11 NIV). Elijah's life had been a whirlwind of activity. He had been so impetuous, so driven, so determined, thrusting himself into the palace of ungodly kings, blowing through Israel like a tornado from God. He left the earth as he lived on the earth—in a whirlwind.

We tend to focus on the spectacular departure, but verse 12 matters more. "Elisha saw this" (NIV). Fifty prophets followed at a distance. They saw Elijah and Elisha together, and suddenly Elijah disappeared. I think it means that all they saw was Elijah disappear. They had no idea what had happened. It was only Elisha whose eyes were opened to see the flaming horses and the flaming chariot. It was only Elisha who saw his master being taken away in the whirlwind. "If you see me," Elijah said. There is the kind of seeing with the eyes, and there is the seeing with the eyes of the heart. It is possible to have 20/20 vision on the outside and be totally blind on the inside. *You can live eighty years with perfect vision and be totally blind to spiritual reality.* That's why Paul prays in Ephesians 1:18 that the "eyes of your heart may be enlightened." You could go to Sunday school all your life, you could even attend a Christian college or go to seminary, and the eyes of your heart could be tightly shut. Just going through the motions doesn't guarantee the eyes of your heart will be open.

Seeing the Invisible

Hebrews 11:27 contains a phrase that helps us understand this principle. Speaking of Moses' willingness to leave the riches of Egypt to live in the wilderness with his own people, the writer says, "He persevered because he saw him who is invisible" (NIV). *That's one of the most remarkable and revealing statements in the entire Bible.* It appears to be an impossibility. How do you "see" an invisible person? If you can be seen, you are not invisible. God was invisible, and yet Moses "saw" him. How? Two words. "By faith." *Moses had faith, and his faith gave him sight.* And he saw the God who is invisible. *Faith sees what is really there even though others see nothing at all.* Faith believes what is true even though others don't believe it at all. By faith we see reality, which means we see beyond the world around us. But that concept should not seem strange at all. After all, the most beloved hymn in the world ("Amazing Grace") contains this line, "I once was lost but now am found, was blind but now I see."

By faith we see what others do not see. Have you ever looked at one of those 3-D pictures that contain hidden images? When you first look at the picture, all you see are wavy lines or dots or perhaps marbles or stars or pieces of fruit. But if you look at the picture up close, and if you throw your eyes out of focus and turn your head a bit cockeyed, suddenly out jumps Mozart's head or a dancing girl or a giant bird. Since I have less-than-perfect eyesight,

I have trouble with 3-D pictures. Usually the only thing I can see is a bunch of lines or something that looks vaguely like a head of cabbage. To my consternation, Marlene can almost always see the "hidden" image. *But just because I can't see it doesn't mean it isn't there.* It's not as if Mozart's head suddenly appears out of nowhere. It was there all along. The "hidden" image is there whether I see it or not. Suddenly you saw what was always there. It's the same way with the life of faith. *The "hidden world" of eternal reality is there whether we see it or not.* And by faith we "see" it even though the people of the world do not.

Our Experience Determines Our Persuasion

This principle has many applications. Not long ago I heard a speaker say that "our experience determines our persuasion." He then applied that to followers of other religions by saying that he didn't get mad at Muslims or Buddhists or Hindus or the many secularists we meet every day. Why get mad at them? *If they truly believe what they claim to believe, it's because they've had an experience that determines their persuasion.* Years ago I learned that "your experience will always beat my doctrine." I can't use logic to destroy your experience, at least not if it truly means something important to you. We've all tried arguing people into the kingdom of God, and it doesn't work. You can't convince someone that Jesus loves them by swearing at them or threatening them or raising your voice in anger. Instead of getting angry at those whose beliefs are radically different, we should pray for God to give them an experience of the truth. Only then will they be persuaded to believe differently.

It happens that I am writing these words from an apartment in Beijing, China. Two days ago I spoke to a small group of Christian leaders and answered their questions. One woman wanted to know how to help a friend who does not know Christ. She has tried to help her, but nothing seems to work. I told her to do three things. First, remain her friend. You can't help someone if you will not talk to them. Second, drop "seeds of truth" into your conversations with her. Don't argue, and don't try to convince her all at once. Third, keep on praying because only God can truly change the heart. *Our words can only go so far, but God's Spirit can melt the hardest heart.* And I asked her, "Do you get angry at people who are blind because they can't see the color green?" No, you don't. If you can't see it, you can't see it. Getting angry makes things worse, not better. Since it is Satan who blinds the minds of unbelievers (2 Cor. 4:4), we must pray that God will open their eyes to see the truth. They will never believe what they do not see, and they will never see until the eyes of the heart are opened, and only God can do that. But God *can* do it, which is why we must pray and keep on praying.

Elijah said, "You can have the power if you see me depart." He didn't just mean if you visually see me, but if God gives you spiritual sight to understand, if he opens the eyes of your heart.

How do I know God answered that prayer? Not because Elisha parted the Jordan with Elijah's cloak. I know it because of the wonderful story that takes place in 2 Kings 6:8–17 when Elisha and his servant are in Dothan and the armies of the king of Aram have completely surrounded them. It's a hopeless situation. Though the servant despairs, Elisha tells him not to worry because "those who are with us are more than those who are with them" (v. 16 NIV). Then Elisha prays, "O LORD, open his eyes so he may see" (v. 17 NIV). When his eyes were opened, the servant saw the armies of God arrayed in the clouds above the Aramean army. It is a great advance spiritually to have your eyes opened to see spiritual reality, to understand that this world is not the only world. When the eyes of the heart are opened, you understand that the unseen world is the real world, the only one that matters.

Elijah's Lasting Legacy

So now one prophet is taken and one prophet is left, showing us that the battle goes on. The church triumphant rejoices in heaven while the church militant on earth continues the battle.

Elisha saw spiritual reality. He saw behind the scenes. At the end of the story, three things happen in quick succession:

1. He saw Elijah depart.
2. He picked up his cloak.
3. He took the cloak to the Jordan River, and he said, "Where is the Lord, the God of Elijah?"

Why did he do that? Elisha was on the east bank of the Jordan. His ministry lay on the western side. Between him and his divine calling flowed the muddy waters of the Jordan River. *He had to get across to enter into God's assignment for his life.* There was no better time than the present to find out if God would be with him as he had been with Elijah. Don't you think it took courage to take that cloak and hit the Jordan River? He had seen Elijah separate the waters, but would the same thing happen for him? Elijah is gone, but is Elijah's God gone also? That's always the great question.

Where is the Lord God of Luther?

Where is the Lord God of Calvin?

Where is the Lord God of Jonathan Edwards?

Where is the Lord God of Charles Haddon Spurgeon?

Where is the Lord God of J. Hudson Taylor?

Where is the Lord God of D. L. Moody?

Where is the Lord God of Billy Sunday?

Where is the Lord God of Jim Elliott?

It took faith to take that same cloak and hit the water, not knowing what was about to happen. It took courage to do that. It was necessary. Elisha had to do it.

He had to do it.

That couldn't happen while Elijah was still on the earth. *Elijah had to go in order for Elisha to arise.* I think these days a lot about my sons. At this writing they are twenty-seven, twenty-five, and twenty-two years old. There is no such thing as hand-me-down faith. *Every generation must discover God's power on its own.* My three sons can't live on my faith. They have to find their own.

Josh has to find his own faith.

Mark has to see for himself.

Nick has to get it on his own.

Elijah had to leave in order for Elisha to take up his ministry. It is the same in every generation. Leaders rise, lead, fight the battle for God, and then at the appointed hour, they move off the scene to be replaced by others whom God has raised up.

God Names His Own Successors

Now we come to the final turn in the road. *Elijah is in heaven, and he's alive and well today.* Hundreds of years later the Lord said through Malachi, "I will send you the prophet Elijah before that great and dreadful day of the LORD comes." (Mal. 4:5 NIV). Four hundred years later, Jesus said of John the Baptist, "He is the Elijah who was to come" (Matt. 11:14 NIV). He meant that John the Baptist had come in the spirit and power of Elijah (Luke 1:17). And later Elijah appeared on the Mount of Transfiguration with Jesus, Peter, and John (Mark 9:2–8). That means he is still alive today.

So if this were your last day, how would you spend it? What would you do? For those who know the Lord, death holds no fear. Our little time on planet Earth zips by, and then we fly away. We're here today and gone tomorrow. Here is the wonderful final word from Elijah's life.

Elijah went to heaven.

Elisha carried on his work.

God's work goes on.

It goes on because God goes on.

He was here before we arrived, and he will be here long after we are gone. Nothing of God dies when a man of God dies. When Elijah went to heaven, God was still the same. When Elisha died, God was still the same. We like to say when our loved ones die, "It will never be the same." And it's true. Life for us will never be the same with our loved ones gone. But our God is in heaven; he changes not. The world doesn't revolve around you and me, and it doesn't depend on our personal presence.

Psalm 100:5 tells us that God's "faithfulness continues through all generations" (NIV). It literally means "from generation to generation." Exodus 20:6 tells us that God shows "his love to a thousand generations" (NIV) of those who love him. If we assume that a biblical generation lasts approximately forty years, this means God's love lasts at least 40,000 years. And since this promise was given to Moses at Mount Sinai approximately 3,500 years ago, we may safely conclude that God's faithful love will continue at least another 36,500 years. That is to say, in 3,500 years we are not yet even 10 percent of the way through the length of God's love. But surely that is not literal, you say. Indeed, it is not. But it is not purely figurative either. It's a way of showing us that God's love and faithfulness go far beyond any human understanding. Suppose we line up a grandfather, a father, a son, a grandson, and a great-grandson on the platform. Psalm 100:5 tells us that what God is to the grandfather, he will be to the father. What he is to the father, he will be to the son. What he is to the son, he will be to the grandson. What he is to the grandson, he will be to the great-grandson. And so it goes across the centuries. Generations come and go, one after the other. Only God remains forever.

I am so glad that God's faithfulness transcends the generations. At the moment I am fifty-three years old heading for . . . what? fifty-five? sixty? seventy-five? Maybe eighty or even ninety years old if God blesses me with long life. But I won't live forever. As the years roll by, I find myself realizing how much of my life is wrapped up in my three boys. Yesterday they were in grade school; today they are almost grown up; and tomorrow they will be grandfathers. Will God still take care of them? What about their children? and their grandchildren? Will God still be there for them? *The answer is yes because God's faithfulness doesn't depend on me but on the character of God that spans the generations.* That means I don't have to stay alive to ensure that my boys will be OK. God will see to that. After I am gone from this earth, and even if all my prayers have not been answered, I can trust God to take care of my boys. What a comfort this is. I can do my best to help my boys while I'm here; and after I'm gone, God's faithfulness will continue for them and for their grandchildren, and even for their great-grandchildren.

Elijah departs for heaven.

Elisha picks up his mantle and carries on his work.

God names his own successors.

The Lord God of Elijah is also the Lord God of Elisha.

We come and go, but our God spans the generations.

Where is the Lord God of Elijah? I've got good news for you. He's still here. The first words out of Elijah's mouth were "As the LORD, the God of Israel, lives" (1 Kings 17:1 NIV). The Lord God of Elijah is our God today.

So I leave you with the question that I started with. Where is the Lord God of Elijah? He's still here. Where are the Elijahs of the Lord God in our own generation?

CONCLUSION

Several years ago my older brother took me to visit a cemetery outside Florence, Alabama, near the remains of an antebellum mansion called Forks of Cypress. The mansion was built in the 1820s by James Jackson, an early settler of northwest Alabama. My brother and I walked among the ruins of the mansion and then crossed the country road into the dense forest on the other side. After a quarter-mile we found the Jackson family cemetery. There is no sign marking the spot, only a five-foot high stone wall surrounding about fifty graves. Inside we found a tall marker over James Jackson's grave with a long inscription extolling his virtues, which were many.

As I walked along, my eyes fastened on the marker for one of his sons. There was a name, a date of birth, a date of death, and this simple five-word epitaph: "A man of unquestioned integrity."

Five words to sum up an entire life. Sixty-plus years distilled into five words. But, oh, what truth they tell.

"A man of unquestioned integrity." I cannot think of a better tribute.

It could have been written about Elijah. He, too, was a man of unquestioned integrity.

As we wrap up our journey through the life of God's mountain man, let's pause to consider two facts about Elijah from the New Testament. *First, Elijah was a lot like us.* When James wanted to encourage his readers to pray fervently, he used this illustration: "Elijah was a man just like us. He prayed earnestly that it would not rain, and it did not rain on the land for three and a half years. Again he prayed, and the heavens gave rain, and the earth produced its crops" (James 5:17–18 NIV).

Ponder that first sentence for a moment. "Elijah was a man like us." It's easy to argue with James when you think of all that Elijah did. He was a man of extremes, never settling for the moderate middle. When Elijah was at his best, he called down fire from heaven and defeated 850 false prophets. When Elijah was at his worst, he ran across the desert and hid in a cave on Mount Horeb. He did nothing by halves, nothing the easy way.

Talk about life on the edge! He was on the edge half the time and over it the rest of the time. What about that story of Elijah laying himself on the body of a dead child and praying for God to bring him back to life? Most of us can't imagine doing something like that. But then we're not like Elijah. Or are we?

The King James Version says that Elijah was a man of "like passions." He means that Elijah was not some superhuman man in a category far beyond the rest of us mere mortals. Elijah experienced all the emotions of life—joy, sorrow, victory, defeat, frustration, exultation, encouragement, discouragement, anger, forgiveness, despair, and relief. We face a twofold danger when we study a life of great accomplishment. On one hand we tend to canonize a man, treating him as if he were exempt from the normal temptations of life. It is easy to chisel Elijah's head on some religious Mount Rushmore and say, "There never was such a man before or since." Or we may focus on a great man's weaknesses and infirmities, concentrating on his failures, faults, and foibles, exposing every sin and every foolish mistake so that in the end he seems not very great at all. We pull him down into the muck and mire of ordinary life until the luster of his greatness has disappeared underneath the veneer of his frailty. All the heroes of the Bible had their weaknesses, and Elijah was no exception. And that is one reason we are drawn to such a man. God used him in spite of his weaknesses.

After his greatest victory, Elijah ran away.

He ran away!

And God had to go and find him.

And talk him back into his senses.

Then God used him again.

That's a good story because it's our story. We've all run away under pressure. We've given up, thrown in the towel, quit the race, caved in when the heat was on.

No one is strong all the time.

We're all made from the same clay.

Elijah's story is our story because Elijah's God is our God too. Just as he came after Elijah, he comes after you and me again and again and again.

He doesn't know when to quit.

He doesn't accept our letter of resignation.

He finds us, calls us, refines us, rebukes us, encourages us, and refits us. Then he commissions us all over again.

What an amazing God we serve. He's the real hero of Elijah's story. We're just like Elijah, and he's just like us, his God is our God, and that's good news.

There is one final thought we need to keep in mind. *Elijah was a lot like Jesus.* At first glance that may seem wrong because Elijah made mistakes and Jesus was sinless. But consider this. Elijah and Jesus were both sent by God. Both were misunderstood by their contemporaries. Both spent time alone in the wilderness. Both worked miracles. Both men spoke the truth. Both of them riled the religious and political establishment of their day. Both of them ascended into heaven—Elijah in a whirlwind and Jesus rising through the clouds. It should not surprise us that some of the common people thought Jesus was the second coming of Elijah (Matt. 16:13) or that when Jesus cried out on the cross, some thought he was calling for Elijah (Matt. 27:47). Nor should we be surprised that Elijah appeared along with Moses during the transfiguration (Matt. 17:3).

Elijah's life stands out in bold relief, like a granite colossus that dominates the landscape for miles around. There was no one like him before or since. Love him or hate him, you could not ignore him. He single-handedly reversed the tide of immorality and idolatry in Israel. He faced down a wicked king and changed the course of a nation. For a brief, shining moment, he brought his countrymen back to God. Even Elisha, his God-appointed successor, did not do what Elijah had done. No wonder the Jews revered Elijah. There never was another man like him. He stands alone in biblical history. Though he lived hundreds of years before Christ, he lived and ministered in the power of the Lord. Study Elijah, learn to be like him, follow his steps, and he will lead you to Jesus.

As I ponder his life and legacy, I am reminded of the words of the great American patriot, Edward Everett Hale:

I am only one man.

But I am one.

I cannot do everything.
But I can do something.
What I can do, I ought to do.
What I ought to do,
By the grace of God,
I will do.

Let me wrap things up by encouraging you to pray that "dangerous" prayer I mentioned in chapter 1: "Lord, do things I'm not used to." It's simple and profound; and because it goes to the root of life, it's a radical prayer. If you're scared to pray that way, that probably means you need that prayer more than you know.

"Lord, do things I'm not used to."

Elijah prayed like that. He was one man wholly dedicated to God in a generation when most people were dedicated to evil. Though far from perfect, he left a mark the world remembers almost three thousand years later. He did what he could, while he could, and he did not shirk his duty. When he had a chance to make a difference, he did. And he didn't worry too much about who was with him and who was against him. He figured that one man plus God was enough. He was right.

What a man!

What a God he served!

Elijah still speaks today because Elijah's God still lives today.

Notes

Introduction

1. Jeannette Clift George, *Troubling Deaf Heaven* (Nashville: Broadman & Holman, 2005), 28.

Chapter 1, God's Mountain Man

1. M. Ferguson, cited by Tom Holmes, in "Finding Their Way, after Ray," *Wednesday Journal Online*, June 20, 2006, www.wjinc.com (accessed July 26, 2006).

2. You can find those sermons online at www.keep believing.com/sermons.

3. "When Gay Activists Came to Calvary," *Leadership Journal*, Winter 2005.

4. Daniel Eisenberg, "What's at Stake in the Fight," *Time Magazine*, July 11, 2005.

5. Cited by Brian Bill, "Running on Empty," Pontiac Bible Church, September 19, 2001.

Chapter 2, Dry Brook University

1. F. B. Meyer, *Elijah and the Secret of His Power*, www.bible teacher.org (accessed July 28, 2006).

2. Ibid.

3. *The Elizabeth Elliott Newsletter*, July–August 2000.

4. Meyer, *Elijah and the Secret of His Power.*

Chapter 3, Elijah and the Ravens

1. Some of the material in this chapter comes from a sermon by Leith Anderson, "Ravens—God's Special Birds," Wooddale Church, Eden Prairie, Minn., August 16–17, 2003.

2. Tim O'Hearn, "Ravens in the Bible," http://minutes withmessiah.tripod.com/minutes/raven.html (accessed July 28, 2006).

3. Sermon by C. H. Spurgeon, "God's Care of Elijah," *Metropolitan Tabernacle Pulpit*, vol. 57, 510–11, Ages Software.

Chapter 4, Empty Barrel Graduate School

1. William H. Pape, *China Travail* (Wheaton, Ill.: The Evangelical Alliance Mission, 1975), 11–12.

2. Leonard J. Vander Zee, "The Ravens and the Widow," South Bend Christian Reformed Church, July 2, 2000, www.sbcrc.org/sermons/2000.07.02.html (accessed July 28, 2006).

Chapter 5, Resurrection Hospital

1. F. B. Meyer, *Elijah and the Secret of His Power*, www.bible teacher.org (accessed July 28, 2006).

2. A. W. Pink, *The Life of Elijah*, chapter 10, www.pbminis tries.org/books/pink/Life_of_Elijah/elijah_10.htm (accessed July 28, 2006).

Chapter 6, Obadiah: A Good Man in a Hard Place

1. F. B. Meyer, *Elijah and the Secret of His Power*, www.bible teacher.org (accessed July 28, 2006).

2. C. H. Spurgeon, "Early Eminent Piety," *Metropolitan Tabernacle Pulpit*, vol. 30, 709, Ages Software.

3. http://washingtoninst.org/quotables (accessed July 28, 2006).

4. Ibid.

Chapter 7, Baal Buster

1. Charles R. Swindoll, *Elijah: A Man of Heroism and Humility* (Nashville: Word Publishing, 2000), 75.

2. Quote found at www.birkeyblog.com, entry for July 18, 2006 (accessed July 28, 2006).

3. Alfred Edersheim, "Ahab, King of Israel," *Bible History, Old Testament*, vol. VI, http://philologos.org/__eb-bhot/vol_VI/ch01.htm (accessed July 28, 2006).

4. Ibid.

5. Cited by Peter Robinson in "The Corner" on *National Review Online*, January 17, 2004.

Chapter 8, Prophet on the Run

1. Lisa Marie Gibson, "Am I Depressed?" http://ohioline.osu.edu/ss-fact/0196.html (accessed July 28, 2006).

2. C. H. Spurgeon, *Lectures to My Students*, vol. 1, Lecture 11, page 171, Ages Software.

3. Ibid., 176.

Chapter 9, How to Help a Caveman

1. Wayne Biddle, "Anger: Rage Beneficial," *Johns Hopkins Magazine*, September 2005, http://www.jhu.edu/~jhumag/0905web/anger1.html (accessed July 28, 2006).

2. Ibid.

3. See www.gohubbard.com (accessed July 28, 2006).

4. F. W. Robertson, "Elijah," October 13, 1850. www.fwrobertson.com (accessed July 28, 2006).

5. Ibid.

6. C. H. Spurgeon, "Exposition of Psalm 42," *Metropolitan Tabernacle Pulpit*, vol. 60, 470, Ages Software.

Chapter 10, Burning the Plow

1. Some of the material in this chapter comes from a sermon by Amy Butler, "The Apprentice," Calvary Baptist Church,

Washington, D.C., June 27, 2004, www.calvarydc.com/ sermons04june27.html (accessed July 28, 2006).

Chapter 11, Payday Someday

1. The title of this chapter, and part of its content, comes from a famous sermon with the same title by R. G. Lee. He preached his sermon on this passage more than one thousand times. When I was about eleven years old, I heard him preach it at the First Baptist Church of Russellville, Alabama. I don't remember much about the sermon except that he slapped the back of one hand into the palm of the other hand repeatedly to illustrate the story of a condemned man walking on death row. I couldn't improve on the title so I decided to borrow it in tribute to the man who made it famous a generation ago. You can find the sermon online at www.newsforchristians.com/clser1/lee-rg001.html (accessed July 28, 2006).

Chapter 12, Is There No God?

1. See www.canrc.org/resources/bop/hcat/index.html (accessed July 28, 2006).

2. See www.cyberhymnal.org/htm/l/b/lbelongs.htm (accessed July 28, 2006).

Chapter 13, Chariots of Fire

1. Peggy Noonan, "You'd Cry Too If It Happened to You," *Fortune*, September 14, 1992. Archived at www.peggynoonan. com/article.php?article=294 (accessed July 28, 2006).

SPECIAL NOTE

If you would like to contact the author, you can reach him in the following ways:

By letter:

Ray Pritchard

1176 Morning Glory Circle

Tupelo, Mississippi 38801

By e-mail: Ray@keepbelieving.com

Via the Internet: www.keepbelieving.com